BOSTON IRISH

PHOTOGRAPHY BY BILL BRETT

FOREWORD BY DAVID McCULLOUGH
TEXT BY CAROL BEGGY

Boston, Irish
Published by:
Three Bean Press, LLC
P.O. Box 5
Millis, MA 02054
info@threebeanpress.com • www.threebeanpress.com

Publishers Cataloging-in-Publication Data
Brett, Bill
Boston, Irish / by Bill Brett. Carol Beggy.
p. cm.
Summary: Photographer Bill Brett captures and celebrates Boston's Irish-American heritage and community
in this compendium of more than 260 black-and-white portraits.

ISBN 978-0-9903315-2-0.
[1. Boston—Nonfiction. 2. Massachusetts—Nonfiction. 3. Portraits—Nonfiction. 4. Photography—Nonfiction.
5. Irish—Nonfiction. 6. Irish-Americans—Nonfiction. 7. Bill Brett—Nonfiction. 8. David McCullough—Nonfiction.]
I. Beggy, Carol. II. Title.
LCCN information is available for this title.

Printed in the USA by Lifetouch through Four Colour Print Group, Louisville, Kentucky.

10 9 8 7 6 5 4 3 2 1

Additional photography credits:
St. Patrick's Day, 1968 © George Riley
Cardinal Seán P. O'Malley and Jack Connors © Kerry Brett
Conan O'Brien © Kerry Brett
Dropkick Murphys © Kerry Brett

Cover and book design by Julie Kelly, Three Bean Press

DEDICATION

This book is dedicated to the author's mother, Mary Ann (Brennan) Brett, in appreciation for what she, and those who preceded and followed her from Ireland, did to help make Boston the city it is today. Mary Ann Brennan was born on April 20, 1903, in a two-room house in the small County Sligo village of Achonry, Ballymote. The youngest of five children born to Margaret McManus and Patrick Brennan, she was adored by her brothers, John, Michael, Thomas, and Pat James.

Ireland was a place of political turmoil and civic unrest as Mary Ann was growing up; many of the Irish were intent on loosing forever the grip of the imperial British on their homeland. Her brother Michael was a captain in the Irish Republican Army during the Irish War of Independence (1919-1921), and, during those years, she helped him by serving as a courier delivering currency and information from post to post for the IRA. Because of her youth, the British didn't suspect her of being an active patriot as so many Irish nationals were at that time. She was never stopped or questioned.

Mary Ann's parents died young, and, at age 23, her future seemed set for the rest of her life: Remain at home to clean, cook, work the farm, and, in general, take care of her brothers. But that was not the life they envisioned for their little sister; she deserved something more promising. So they pooled their money and purchased a second-class ticket for her to cross the Atlantic to live with an aunt in Philadelphia. One of her cousins never forgot the sight of her dancing around the kitchen, twirling the Irish Republic's tricolors while clutching her ticket to the land across the sea, the United States of America.

Her aunt passed away a few years later, after which Mary Ann made her way to Salem, Massachusetts, where she met and married Henry J. Brett, who also had emigrated from County Sligo. They soon made their way to Boston to raise their family, which eventually numbered six children: Jack, Harry, Peg (McCobb), Mary (McCarthy), Bill, and Jim. Jack was 76 when he passed on and joined his parents.

A quiet, shy, hardworking, religious, and loving mother, Mary Ann taught her children by example; do as I do, not just as I say. In the 1930s and 1940s, she worked overnight shifts, cleaning floors in the big banks in downtown Boston while forming some wonderful friendships. All these women were grateful to have jobs where they could be with their children during the day. Mary Ann was a dedicated stay-at-home mother; her only activities outside her home were monthly Sodality and Legion of Mary meetings at St. Margaret's Church in Dorchester.

Mary Ann Brett was a lady of grace and dignity, a caring and loving grandmother, and a woman of strong faith whose church and children were central to her life. On her death at age 77 on March 28, 1981, she left a legacy of great love to her six children, 17 grandchildren, and 16 great-grandchildren, one of whom—the beloved Christopher Grimes—recently joined her in heaven at the age of eight. A seventeenth great-grandchild is on the way.

A lady full of hope, Mary Ann, who was immensely proud of her Irish heritage and so grateful for her United States citizenship, shared that hope with many others during her long life. She never forgot how it felt to be poor, and, as a tribute to that wonderful sense of generosity and charity, her children have memorialized her in perpetuity with their establishment of the Mary Ann Brett Food Pantry at St. Margaret's Church in Blessed Mother Teresa Parish in Dorchester.

"Believe that further shore
Is reachable from here.
Believe in miracle
And cures and healing wells."
—*Seamus Heaney*

FOREWORD
By David McCullough

With this magnificent and altogether good-hearted book, Bill Brett once again provides us with an historic treasure. History, let us not forget, is much more than dates and statistics and the tenants of obscure provisos. History is human. "When in the course of human events," our Declaration of Independence begins and the operative word is "human."

In the faces of the many photographed by Bill Brett over the past 50 years are to be found a half century of the history of Boston—a collection such as we have for no other city in America. The portraits in the pages that follow, along with the biographical information provided by Carol Beggy, leave no doubt as to the appealing individuality and the important parts played by the Irish of Boston.

Boston, Irish is a grand gallery of a whole cast of varied characters. Here are to be found politicians (naturally), physicians, musicians and electricians; teachers, war heroes, chief executive officers and a chauffeur; police officers, firemen, restaurateurs, developers and builders; reporters, scholars, writers and painters; priests and nuns, college presidents and hotel managers, famous athletes, the chief engineer of the Boston Water and Sewer Commission and the first woman to head the Boston Public Library. And many more.

It is important also, I think, to note that the Irish Americans in Bill Brett's portraits include a considerable number who have come to Boston from elsewhere in the country, as indeed have I. Like Carol Beggy, I grew up in Pittsburgh, where my Protestant Irish ancestors first settled in the 18th century.

If I had to pick a favorite photograph among this collection, I suppose it would be that of Sister Evelyn Hurley. Out for a stroll in the splendid hat, coat and scarf she hand-knitted herself. And if not her, then the Boston Police Gaelic Column of Pipes and Drums.

There is a great deal to love about Boston, so much that is not to be found in other cities. One of them surely is the lively presence of Irish in abundance. Another is Bill Brett.

INTRODUCTION

By Kevin Cullen

It was probably only a matter of time before Bill Brett created this book. It ended up coinciding with the 50th anniversary of the first photograph he had published in *The Boston Globe*. But he did it for other reasons, and, if I had to guess, I'd say the biggest reason was his mother.

Mary Ann Brett, who left Ireland for America without much more in her pocket than hope, had a difficult first pregnancy. Her son Jack was born with a severe mental disability. A paternalistic doctor in Boston took her aside and suggested she put Jack in an institution and not have any more children. Mary Ann Brett had a sixth-grade education, and she was just off the boat from Ireland. But she looked that allegedly learned man in the eye and said, "He will not be going to an institution. He is going home. And I'm going to have more children, and they will provide love for him, and we will love him as a family, and thank you very much."

And that's just what Mary Ann Brett did. She went on to have five more children, including our Bill. And the Brett kids did just what their mother predicted, loving and taking care of Jack, who taught them more about love and loyalty and compassion than any doctor could. Jack had a good life, richer than many. He was 76 when he died. He is buried right next to his mother in Cedar Grove Cemetery in Dorchester, the neighborhood where the Bretts and so many Irish immigrants made their homes.

Mary Ann Brett represented the best of the Boston Irish, and if it was her son Bill whose eyes framed these photographs, it was her sensibilities that inform them, which give this book its narrative arc and context. Her life, a life of struggle, was the immigrant's challenge. Her children's lives, of assimilation and success, are the immigrant's dream.

Because of its relatively small size, Boston has never had the ethnic diversity of, say, New York. But its immigration history, as well as its topography, was always a metaphor for the promise and peril of America's melting pot. It was the "City Upon a Hill," as the first governor of Massachusetts Bay Colony, John Winthrop, put it, using a biblical phrase.

The Protestant Englishmen who settled Boston quickly established the same kind of hierarchical society they had professed to despise in England. They had Boston in some sort of working order when successive potato crops in Ireland failed in the 1840s. There had been a small Irish population in Boston before, but the Irish who began to arrive in huge numbers late in that decade were often diseased and always desperate. And, perhaps just as bad, if not worse, as far as the Brahmins who had settled the city were concerned, they were Catholic.

The Famine Irish had it very hard at first. They had to figure out a way to survive in a town that wasn't welcoming or inclusive. When their children couldn't get into university, they appealed to the Jesuits and founded Boston College. When they couldn't get the political establishment to represent their interests, they began pushing their own politicians. The Boston Irish took to politics the way ducks in the Public Garden take to water.

It is said that in Boston we really only care deeply about three things: politics, sports, and revenge. That's very Irish. In just a few generations, the Boston Irish went from being a put-upon minority to becoming the city's dominant ethnic group. First, they were the city's cops and firefighters. Access to education pushed them beyond the typical jobs, and soon they were in the mercantile class, and then the boardrooms, and then the white-shoe law firms downtown. They elbowed their way into the golf clubs and downtown social clubs where a century before they had been present only as servants.

Boston remains the only large city in America where the Irish are the biggest ethnic group, still more than a fifth of the population, congregated mostly in South Boston, West Roxbury, Brighton and a few remaining neighborhoods in Dorchester. The suburbs that ring the city are in many cases the most populous Irish-American enclaves in the country. They don't call the South Shore "The Irish Riviera" for nothing. While other cities that were initially swamped with Famine refugees saw the Irish assimilate and move to exurbia, the Boston Irish have stuck close to the city. In metropolitan Boston, they remain the dominant ethnic group in politics and business. And they still flood the police and fire departments, not just in Boston but in the entire metropolitan area.

Still, the Boston Irish of today are far different than those first few generations who got off the coffin ships or, in some cases, never made it past a grave on Deer Island. The Irish make up a smaller proportion of the population in Boston than just a few generations ago, and so they have learned to make alliances, and real friendships, with immigrant groups newer to the city.

One of the most striking photos in this book is of three priests in Dorchester—Doc Conway, Jack Ahern, and Dan Finn. Father Dan is Irish born. Father Jack and Doc—Doc would laugh at me if I called him Father Doc—are of Irish stock and certainly Irish sensibilities. But their flocks are hardly Irish. Doc learned Portuguese so he could help the Cape Verdean kids on Meetinghouse Hill. Father Jack and Father Dan are more often tending to people of color than people with the map of Ireland on their face.

Throughout most of the 20th century, a mayor of Irish extraction occupied Boston City Hall. Tom Menino ended that run in 1994, when he defeated Bill Brett's brother, Jim, for the mayoralty. Menino stepped down after 20 years and was replaced by Marty Walsh, a Dorchester guy and son of Irish immigrants. But describing Marty Walsh as an Irish pol is like calling Seamus Heaney an Irish poet: It's accurate at one level, but very misleading and incomplete.

Marty didn't get elected by the Irish vote. He got elected by white folks and black folks and brown folks and yellow folks and by people who, like Marty himself, had parents whose first language wasn't English. Marty's mom, Mary, and his dad, John, spoke Gaelic in their homes in Ireland. After they immigrated to Boston in the 1950s, they spoke Irish in their three-decker on Taft Street in Savin Hill so that Marty and his brother Johnny wouldn't know what they were talking about.

The point is, describing someone as Boston Irish doesn't mean the same thing it used to. It's much broader, much wider, much deeper. Linda Dorcena Forry, the state senator from Dorchester who now presides over the St. Patrick's Day breakfast and political roast, is Boston Irish. She also happens to be a black Haitian married to an Irish-American guy from Dorchester and can belt out *The Wild Colonial Boy* with the best of them.

Today, the term Boston Irish says more about someone's culture and ethos than their ethnicity and race.

Thomas H. O'Connor, the eminent late historian at Boston College whose portrait graces these pages, explained this metamorphosis in his book *The Boston Irish, A Political History*.

"They are no longer the immigrants and exiles of the Famine era. The Boston Irish have become people of education, culture, and refinement. To a great extent, in their prolonged struggle for survival and achievement, they did turn Boston into an Irish city. For that reason, they now have a special obligation to give back to that city the benefit of the skills, the associations, and the resources they have acquired.

"In this way, they can help preserve the kind of cultivated and responsive community John Winthrop envisioned in 1630, so that new immigrant peoples and their families can share the many advantages of the 'City Upon a Hill,' where the Boston Irish prospered so well, accomplished so much, and endured for so long."

Bill Brett feels the same way as Tom O'Connor, a man he deeply admired. The story of the Boston Irish holds hope and promise for all other immigrant groups, though he is the first to admit that the Irish had a huge advantage in being white and speaking English. He is also the first to admit that the Irish should remember their history, that whatever terrible things are said about immigrants today were said about the Irish 150 years ago.

A quarter century ago, after Bruce Bolling became the first black president of the Boston City Council, he used his office and power to punish a political rival, maintaining a tradition that stretched back more than a century, when Irish ward bosses used their clout to exact revenge on anyone who challenged the machine.

Not long after he became council president, I sidled up to Bruce at a reception at the Parkman House, the mayor's official residence on Beacon Hill.

"Jesus, Bruce," I said, draping my arm around his shoulder. "A brother finally gets the job, and what's the first thing you do: Whack somebody like you're an Irish pol."

Bruce betrayed a smile, slid his arm around my shoulder, cocked his head toward me in mock incredulity and said, "Kevin, in this town, we're all Irish by osmosis."

Bruce Bolling died in 2012, some 31 years after Mary Ann Brett. But I like the idea of them being in the same place right now, in a realm far different than ours. They were both such decent people. And they were both so Boston Irish.

Boston Police Gaelic Column of Pipes and Drums

They can trace their family roots back to the counties of Cork, Donegal, Dublin, Galway, Leitrim and Mayo, and they represent Boston area law enforcement at many of the biggest events in the region. Since its formation in 1992, the **Boston Police Gaelic Column of Pipes and Drums** has performed at numerous events including on board the *USS Constitution* during the ship's 200th birthday celebration and on the deck of the *USS John F. Kennedy*, when the aircraft carrier was in the harbor as part of Sail Boston. The pipe and drum band has led the St. Patrick's Day parade in South Boston since 1994. They have also been recognized in Ireland, including winning the Patrick J. Murphy Trophy given to the "best bagpipe band" in the Cork City St. Patrick's Day parade. They were in Bantry for the dedication of the statue erected in memory of Chicago Police Chief Francis O'Neill, an immigrant who is credited with saving Irish music at the turn of the 20th century. The members are, from left, in the first row: Patrolman Sean Brundige; Patrolman Paul Boyle; Patrolman Derryl Lawrence; Sergeant Detective Tom Sexton; Patrolman James Barry, the band's president and drum major; Detective Dan Fagan; Sergeant Tom Leahy; Lieutenant John Mayer. Second row: Patrolman John Connelly; Patrolman Tim Ballinger; Patrolman James Walsh; Sergeant Robert Ferguson; Patrolman Edward Boylan; Detective (retired) Edward Walsh, father of James Walsh. Third row: Captain Dennis Dowling; Chief Richard Wells; Sergeant Joe Cheevers; Lieutenant Adrian Troy; Sergeant Eric Krause; Lieutenant Brian Leary.

Kathleen MacNeil

One of 11 children, **Kathleen MacNeil** often refers to her mother as an Irish saint and attributes her success to her mother's work ethic. Kathy grew up just outside of Lowell and was the first in her family to "go away" to college. She studied architectural engineering at Wentworth Institute and received her graduate degree from MIT Center for Real Estate. She has spent the majority of her career managing complex urban real estate projects for Millennium Partner's Boston portfolio. She worked on the restoration of the original Ritz-Carlton (now the Taj), the Ritz-Carlton Boston Common hotel and condominiums on Avery Street, and the new Millennium Place condos. She is managing the Filene's building restoration and the new Millennium Tower, where she was photographed in early 2014. She recently joined Wentworth's board of corporators and is on the Board of Historic Boston. So far she is pleased with the restoration of the 1912 Filene's Building designed by Daniel Burnham, saying it has been "a fascinating look back in history," and she is "proud to be part of the team that has restored it."

Dan McCole

Watercolorist and illustrator **Dan McCole** uses his considerable talent to document familiar Boston scenes and capture the Ireland he remembers. Dan is one of eight children—and the fourth son—born to Phil and Maggie (McGonagle) McCole. Dan's parents emigrated from Co. Donegal with three of his older siblings. Dan has held a number of newspaper jobs over the years; he has worked as an editorial artist for the Boston Herald Traveler, in the Boston Herald advertising department, as founder of the weekly *Weymouth News,* and as editor of the *Boston Irish Echo* before returning to the *Herald.* In 2005, he embarked on a career as a watercolorist and co-owned a gallery in South Boston that closed in 2008. Dan holds free painting classes for children through the South Boston Community Health Center. President and cofounder of the South Boston Arts Association, Dan is chairman of nonprofit South Boston Arts & Cultural Center Task Force, which was organized to explore ways to create a South Boston Arts &

David Marr and Richard Kelleher

One of the city's most notable hoteliers, **Richard Kelleher** (right) helped create the Boston skyline of today over the past three decades, as he has managed more than a dozen Boston area hotels. Rick is CEO of Pyramid Hotel Group, which manages Boston Harbor Hotel, The Residence Inn on Boston Harbor at Tudor Wharf, The Residence Inn Boston Back Bay-Fenway, and 56 other properties in the United States and the Caribbean. Rick is photographed with **David Marr**, the head doorman at the five-star Boston Harbor Hotel—and the hotel's first hire when it opened in 1987. Rick has deep roots in the Irish market town of Macroom in Co. Cork, from whence his great-grandfather emigrated in the late 19th century. Rick's cousins still operate the dairy farm, and Rick and his family have visited there over the years. Rick's grandfather Dennis Kelleher was a Cambridge City Councilor and his father, Richard Kelleher, was a decorated World War II combat medical officer. The Kellehers have been longtime supporters of the Irish American Partnership. Dave was born and raised in South Boston. His great-grandparents Bernard McCabe, from Co. Meath, and Anne (Cooney), from Co. Clare, left Ireland during the potato famine and lived in Somerville. Dave's parents, Marylou (Musco) and Francis Marr, lived in South Boston, where his father grew up. His father was a Vietnam War veteran and a retired colonel in the U.S. Army. Dave went to high school at Thompson Academy in South Boston during the tough years of court-ordered busing in Boston.

The Collinses

Former Ireland Ambassador to the United States **Michael Collins** (center) is shown with Dr. **Michael F. Collins**, chancellor of the University of Massachusetts Medical School, and his son, **Michael Jr.** A Dublin native, the Ambassador was Ireland's representative in Washington, D.C., for six years, the longest tenure in the modern era, until being posted to Berlin in August 2013. Dr. Collins and his son are both graduates of the College of the Holy Cross. The former attended Tufts University School of Medicine, trained in medicine at St. Elizabeth's in Boston, and a decade later served as president of St. Elizabeth's and the Caritas Christi Health System before becoming Chancellor at University of Massachusetts Boston. Michael Jr. worked at State Street Global Advisors prior to joining Dovetail Health and is in the master's of business administration program at Trinity College in Dublin. Dr. Collins' grandparents were from Ireland; his grandfather was a proud Cork man who came to the United States and became a railroad union leader in Scranton, Pennsylvania, and then Norwood, Massachusetts. Dr. Collins has served as chair of the board at Holy Cross and on numerous other educational, health care, and nonprofits, and Michael Jr. has been active in the young professionals group at the American Ireland Fund. When in Ireland, both are treated royally, given that they share a name with the Irish revolutionary and author of the Republic's constitution. They came to know Ambassador Collins during their many visits and interactions with the Irish government, both in the United States and Ireland.

Conan O'Brien

"I live in Los Angeles and an Irishman in Los Angeles is like a penguin in the Lebanon zoo. I don't thrive there," **Conan O'Brien** told those gathered at a 2013 ceremony at Trinity College Dublin's Philosophical Society, where he received an honorary patronage. Conan is a Brookline native who graduated *magna cum laude* from Harvard University, where he was president of the *Harvard Lampoon*. A late–night talk show host since 1993, his *Conan* show can be seen weeknights on the TBS cable network. He is the third of six children born to Dr. Thomas F. O'Brien, a senior physician at Brigham and Women's Hospital and associate professor at Harvard Medical School, and Ruth (Reardon) O'Brien, a former partner at Ropes & Gray, who retired in 1996. The O'Brien family traces its heritage back to Co. Kerry. Conan serves on the John F. Kennedy Library Foundation's board of directors and is honorary chair of the John F. Kennedy Presidential Library Foundation's New Frontier Network.

Raymond L. Flynn, Thomas M. Menino, and Kevin H. White

This photograph was taken by Bill Brett during a shoot for the cover of his first book, *Boston, All One Family*, which was released in 2005. It has become something like Ted Williams's last at-bat at Fenway because a lot of people claim they were there with Bill and the mayors. It was a 15-minute session, and without much ado, Bill picked up the umbrellas on his way to the Public Garden where his subjects, former mayors **Raymond L. Flynn** (left), and **Kevin H. White** and sitting Mayor **Thomas M. Menino**, had gathered. After the now-iconic photograph was taken, Mayor White left to attend a campaign event for his daughter Patricia's run for Boston City Council and Mayor Menino went off on city business. Mayor Flynn served at City Hall from 1984 until his appointment in 1993 as the U.S. Ambassador to the Vatican. He is the fourth of five children born to Stephen L. Flynn, a longshoreman, and Lillian Anne (Kirby) Flynn, both of whom were first generation Americans whose parents emigrated from Co. Galway. Mayor White, who was in office from 1968 to 1984, is one of the dozen men of Irish descent who have served as the city's chief executive. And it was Mayor Menino who, after returning from a trip to Ireland, suggested to the late philanthropist Tom Flatley that he take up the cause of building Boston's Irish Famine Memorial. Menino, who was mayor from 1993 until 2014, an unprecedented five terms, died on October 30, 2014, at age 71.

Sullivan & McLaughlin

After serving in the Marine Corps, **John McLaughlin** (second right) started a small electrical contracting business in 1968. Sullivan & McLaughlin, which is often called "SullyMac," grew to be one of New England's largest union electrical contracting companies. SullyMac continues to be a family-run company led by **John Rudicus** (far left)—who is married to John McLaughlin's daughter Kate—and John McLaughlin's sons **Hugh** (second from left) and **John** (right). The McLaughlins' Dorchester success story begins with their forebear Hughie McLaughlin, who was born in 1899. The eldest of three children, Hughie was raised on a small farm called Ballybreen on the Inishowen Peninsula, Co. Donegal. His wife, Marie Rawdon, was born in 1907 and raised in Moville, Co. Donegal. Hughie and his siblings immigrated to America,

arriving in Boston during the 1920s. After working as a bellhop at the former Statler Hotel, he spent 45 years working as the sexton at St. Peter's Church in Dorchester, a community where he and Marie lived their entire lives. The family established the Ballybreen-Drummaville Charitable Trust, named after the two families' original homesteads, which focuses on enhancing education for underprivileged youths by supporting Cristo Rey Boston High School (in the former St. William's School in Dorchester) and Boston College High School. In 2012, SullyMac partnered with the I.B.E.W. Local 103 to form an "Electrician Volunteer Corp" and deployed more than 100 electricians to assist in completing the construction of the largest hospital in Haiti for the nonprofit Partners in Health.

Pamela McDermott

Pamela McDermott, founder, president, and CEO of McDermott Ventures, is known as one of New England's leading public strategists. But there are still people who remember her for bringing Irish singer John McDermott (no relation) to America in 1996, two years before the Irish Tenors supergroup was launched. In addition to their common last name, the two also bonded over being Scots-Irish. McDermott Ventures is Pam's fourth start-up entrepreneurial firm, which includes McDermott/O'Neill & Associates, the region's largest public affairs and strategic communications firm. She married Boston attorney Terence P. McDermott in 1984, joining his Irish-Catholic family that emigrated from Co. Roscommon, landing in Dorchester. A graduate of the University of Vermont, Pam serves on the board of the university's Foundation. She has also held a number of public policy positions in the City of Boston, the Commonwealth of Massachusetts, and the New England Governors' Conference. Pam made her own foray into Boston politics when she ran unsuccessfully in 1981 for Boston City Council.

Dropkick Murphys

The **Dropkick Murphys** have strong ancestral ties to Ireland and have created new connections as well, performing more than 17 years' worth of live shows there and collaborating with Irish legends such as Shane MacGowan and the late Ronnie Drew. The egalitarian group, which formed in 1996 in the basement of a friend's barbershop, are (from left): **Al Barr**, **Ken Casey**, **Josh "Scruffy" Wallace**, **Ken Brennan**, **James Lynch**, **Jeff DaRosa**, and **Matt Kelly**. The Dropkick Murphys—and their remake of *Tessie*, a 1903 song—became a symbol of the serendipitous luck that followed the Boston Red Sox to the 2004 World Series championship, the team's first in 86 years. The band's song *I'm Shipping Up to Boston* was used over the opening credits of the movie *The Departed*. After winning an Academy Award for his direction of the Boston–set movie, Martin Scorsese was effusive in his praise. "I'm really thankful for the people in Boston who really did a great job, that great group, the Dropkick Murphys," he said backstage. But for singer-guitarist Ken Casey, it all comes back to making music and doing good things. The Dropkick Murphys' foundation, the Claddagh Fund (claddaghfund.org), raises money for Irish charitable causes on both sides of the Atlantic, including the Belvedere Youth Club in Dublin and Springboard-Opportunities in Belfast.

Cardinal Seán P. O'Malley and Jack Connors

Cardinal **Seán P. O'Malley**, OFM Cap, and **Jack Connors** have been called two of the leading voices among the city's Irish-Catholic community. Cardinal Seán, as he asked to be called, eschewing the more formal references, was appointed by Pope John Paul II as Archbishop of Boston in July 2003. Pope Benedict XVI named him Cardinal in 2006. Born in Ohio and raised in Western Pennsylvania, he professed into the Order of Friars Minor Capuchin and was ordained a Catholic priest. With ancestral roots in Westport, Co. Mayo, he has championed the causes of immigrants, including founding Centro Católico Hispano at Catholic University where he taught after receiving his master's and doctorate degrees there. He has filed regular updates since September 2006 on his *Cardinal Seán's Blog*. Jack is a social entrepreneur who has supported an array of civic and philanthropic causes. He is a founding partner of the Boston advertising firm Hill Holliday, who, since his retirement, has focused his efforts at the Connors Family Foundation and on the creation and support of Camp Harbor View. The 12-acre program, run on Boston's Long Island, provides summer programs for children from the city, ages 11 to 14. An Irish American, Jack was raised in Roslindale. In 2012, Jack stepped down from the boards of Brigham and Women's Hospital, Massachusetts General Hospital, and Partners HealthCare after 20 years.

Dr. Martin Dunn

Dr. **Martin Dunn**, the son of a church sexton, made the lessons of his Jesuit educators the guiding principles of his life. A retired oral and maxillofacial surgeon, Marty cofounded Por Christo, a nonprofit medical service organization that has raised millions of dollars to fund dozens of medical missions to help women and children in South America. Alexandra Balcazar, a young orphan from Ecuador who had a debilitating birth defect, is among those Marty has helped. He performed a seven-hour surgery to rebuild the young girl's jaw. Alex was ultimately adopted by Marty and his wife, Carol. Born one of 10 children in Quincy, Marty attended Boston College High School, paying the $180-a-year tuition by doing odd jobs. He remains involved with his alma mater and serves as a trustee. He also worked to pay his own way through Boston College and later Tufts. Marty's father, James J. Dunn, left Kilkenny for America when he was 17 years old.

John F. Fitzgerald and John F. "Jack" Harrington

John F. Fitzgerald (left) and **John F. "Jack" Harrington**, cofounders and principals of Atlantic Associates, a Boston-based IT placement agency, each have connections to some of the city's most prominent Irish leaders from the early 20th century. Born in South Boston, John is named for his ancestor Boston Mayor John F. "Honey Fitz" Fitzgerald, the father of Rose (Fitzgerald) Kennedy and grandfather of President Kennedy. John's branch of the family tree lived in South Boston for five generations, and he continues that connection by serving on the board of the South Boston Boys & Girls Club. Prior to his work at Atlantic, John worked for many years in different management positions at the MBTA and later served as director of the Sewerage Division for the Massachusetts Water Resources Authority. Jack's great-aunt was Julia Harrington Duff. In December 1900, Julia, a mother from Charlestown and former teacher, was the first woman elected to the Boston School Committee. Jack has been involved with many nonprofits in the city, including The Home for Little Wanderers, which supports children in need. Jack led a team to create the Harrington House, named for his parents, John and Patricia, a 16-bed group home serving children ages eight to 15 and their families.

Arthur H. Tobin

Arthur H. Tobin's more than 50-year career in public service will likely never be duplicated. Arthur, the clerk-magistrate at Quincy District Court for 33 years, has held every elected office in Quincy. Arthur has represented the South Shore city as a member of the School Committee, including its chairman, president of the City Council, and in the State House, first as a representative and later as state senator. Arthur served in the U.S. Marine Corps during the Korean War and attended Boston College Law School. His family's roots trace back to the Ireland counties of Cork and Tipperary. His great-grandfather Patrick landed in East Boston, ultimately making his way to Quincy, which has been home to generations of the Tobin family ever since. Once in the Boston area, Arthur's ancestors held some of the familiar jobs for recent immigrants of that time: working as a conductor for the Eastern Massachusetts Street Railway, a model for Filene's department store, and housemaid in a downtown Boston home of a prominent Brahmin family.

Kate Walsh

Boston Medical Center President and CEO **Kate Walsh** began her career in health care as a summer intern at Brookside Health Center in Jamaica Plain. The oldest of five, she grew up in Brookline, in the former Infant Jesus Parish. Her father "was a policeman, and my mom a homemaker…we are pretty much from central casting," Kate says. She attended Yale University, where she received bachelor's and master's degrees in public health. Before her appointment to the Boston Medical Center in 2010, she was executive vice president and chief operating officer of Brigham and Women's Hospital for five years. Her mother's family came from Co. Galway and made Charlestown their new home. Her father's family emigrated from Co. Leitrim to Brookline. Kate says that her favorite part of Ireland is the more remote part of Connemara. "I'm grateful to share a small part of such a special country and culture," she says, "and I'm delighted by curiosity, generosity, humor and zest for life which characterizes the many Irish men and women I've been so fortunate to know."

Susan Kay

For Weymouth Mayor **Susan (Sullivan) Kay** most South Shore towns remind her of Boston's Irish enclaves a half century ago. "In many ways, the Weymouth of today is like the South Boston I grew up in," Sue told *The Boston Globe*. "It's a close-knit place, and the accent is on families, much as it was back then." Sue grew up in an Irish-Catholic family of five in South Boston and attended Catholic schools for 12 years. She worked as the general manager of the *South Boston Tribune* and later for the *Weymouth News*. A longtime resident of Weymouth, Sue was more of an engaged citizen than a traditional politician. She was on the town's Finance Committee, the Appropriations Committee and the Personnel Board before her election to the Board of Selectmen. She was elected as Weymouth's second—and only—woman mayor in 2007. She easily won reelection in 2011.

Mike Sheehan

Family and a sense of place are important to **Mike Sheehan**. He began his career at the age of 15 as sports editor of the *Weymouth News* and is now the CEO of *The Boston Globe*. In the interim, he was an award-winning advertising copywriter and creative director and served as chief creative officer, president, CEO and chairman of Hill Holliday. His paternal grandparents emigrated from Castleisland, Co. Kerry and Glenfarne, Co. Leitrim, in 1922. They met at a Fourth of July party in Quincy shortly thereafter, married, and had their first child, Mike's dad, Frederick, who is shown here in a photograph Mike took of him on Cape Cod. Frederick received the Bronze Star and Purple Heart for his service in World War II, became an attorney, and was appointed State Comptroller at the age of 32. He would later serve as an Assistant Attorney General. (Frederick passed away in 2013.) Mike serves on the Board of Trustees of the American Repertory Theater and helped found The One Fund Boston with Mayor Menino, Jim Gallagher, and Jack Connors within hours of the 2013 Boston Marathon bombings.

Richard B. and Neal F. Finnegan

Richard B. Finnegan (left) and **Neal F. Finnegan**, brothers and Dorchester natives, have made their mark on Boston. Richard graduated from Stonehill College, where he has taught since 1968. An Irish studies scholar and the author of several books on Ireland, Richard's work has focused on international relations. He spent two professional sabbaticals in Ireland—first at University College Dublin and later as an Irish American Cultural Institute research fellow at the Centre for Irish Studies at Galway's National University of Ireland. In 2011, Richard was recognized with a Fulbright Award that took him to the Czech Republic to teach and conduct research comparing Irish and Czech political development. A graduate of Northeastern University's College of Business Administration with a degree in finance, Neal has had a long career in the senior leadership of several Boston financial institutions, including U.S. Trust, Shawmut Bank, and Citizens Bank. A Northeastern trustee since 1989, he served as the board's chairman for 10 years. In 2008, he was the first to be awarded the school's Presidential Medallion, the highest honor bestowed upon a member of the Northeastern community. Active in the community, Neal was an executive member and trustee of WGBH Public Television, past chair of Catholic Charities, and a charter member and director of the Ireland Chamber of Commerce in the United States.

John Fish

Building the Boston Irish Famine Memorial in the heart of the city was not one of Suffolk Construction's largest projects, but for **John Fish**, the company's chairman and CEO, it ranks among his company's most meaningful works. "When I received a call from Boston legend Tom Flatley asking me to participate in this project," John says, "I felt like I had discovered the end of the rainbow." With more than $2 billion in annual revenue, Suffolk Construction is the largest builder in New England. John's great-grandmother Julia Walsh was born in Ireland, and he looks to the life she led after she crossed the Atlantic as an example of how to give back to his community. The Boys & Girls Clubs of Boston and the Boston Green Ribbon Commission are among the nonprofits that he supports. The first non-alumnus to serve as chairman of the Boston College Board of Trustees, John is chairman of Boston 2024 Partnership, the team heading up Boston's bid to host the Olympics and Paralympics in 2024.

Helen Drinan

When she first took a job at BankBoston, **Helen Gannon Drinan**'s father reminded her that its predecessor, The First National Bank of Boston, had a huge sign outside its door discouraging Irish applicants. She went on to work there for 20 years. Now president of Simmons College, Helen (left) has made inclusion a keystone of her tenure at the college in the Fenway. Helen is shown with Simmons alumna **Jill Zarin**, a best-selling author and reality television star. Helen keeps a symbol of her Irish history near to her; the paisley shawl her great-grandmother wore when she emigrated from Ireland during the famine in the mid-19th century, hangs in Helen's office at Simmons. The shawl, which has a Celtic cross in the center, shows signs of wear and mending by Helen's great-grandmother. "When I talk about Simmons College founder John Simmons, who sought to help women struggling with menial work and low wages by providing them with an education to earn an independent livelihood," Helen says, "I think about the many women like my great-grandmother…and how they persevered."

William L. Burke III

Headmaster of St. Sebastian's School since 1990, **William L. Burke III** is the first layman to lead the independent, all-male Catholic school. Bill received a bachelor's degree from Middlebury College, where he was a goaltender on the varsity hockey team, a master's from Boston College, and has studied at Trinity College in Dublin. "My love of all things Irish has ever been manifest," says Bill. "While my father loved the Church, he was never simply Catholic, but, rather, Irish Catholic, and so it has been for me and my six siblings." His three great aunts, who ran a Catholic bookstore in upstate New York, traced the Burke family line to the parish of Moycarkey in Thurles, Co. Tipperary. He is married to child psychologist Dr. Patricia Burke, and they have four sons—all St. Sebastian's men, he notes—William IV '95 (Harvard '99), Daniel '97 (Dartmouth '01, Harvard master's of education '14), Matthew '00 (Middlebury '04), and Sam '04 (Harvard '08, Harvard Business School '13).

Dr. William T. O'Connell

Dr. **William T. O'Connell** dedicated his life to ensuring that those who fled Ireland during "The Great Hunger," traveling on the coffin ships only to die while at the quarantine station in Boston Harbor, are not forgotten. He worked with his wife, Rita, to document the names of the hundreds who died between 1847 and 1850 on Deer Island and are buried at the New Rest Haven Cemetery. Bill, who passed away in January 2014, did not live to see his dream fully realized, but there is a marker on Deer Island recognizing the nearly 20,000 people who were held on the island and the nearly 1,000 who are believed to have died while there from diseases that included typhoid fever, cholera, and dysentery. This immigrant story resonated with Bill, who was the son of Ireland-born parents. He was a member of the Ancient Order of Hibernians in Plymouth and the Knights and Ladies of St. Finbarr.

The Evans Brothers

Boston Police Commissioner **William B. Evans** (far left) is shown here with his brothers—(from left) **John**, **Paul**, **Thomas**, and **James**—at the baseball field in South Boston that is named for their brother Joseph who was struck and killed by a car in 1968 when he was age 11. Their maternal grandmother, Elizabeth Killoran, was born at Flower Hill, Ballymote in Co. Sligo, and their maternal grandfather, John Dineen, was born in Ballylickey, Co. Cork. John arrived in Boston on the *Arabic* on May 3, 1912, and Elizabeth arrived in Boston on the same ship two years later. The couple met through family, and when they married they settled at 3 O Street in the City Point section of South Boston—near where this photograph was taken. The Dineens had eight children and 35 grandchildren. Their descendants now number well over 100. Bill was named interim commissioner by Mayor Menino in November 2013 and appointed commissioner by Mayor Walsh in January 2014. Bill joined the department in 1980 through the cadet program and worked his way up through the ranks to superintendent before heading the department. John retired as a district chief with the Boston Fire Department and is a U.S. Army veteran. Paul served as commissioner of the Boston Police Department from 1993 to 2004. He, too, worked his way up during his tenure, running the department for a period of time that included a 31-year low in violent crime in 2002. Paul is a veteran of the U.S. Marine Corps and served in the Vietnam War. Thomas works for NStar, and James, a U.S. Army veteran, retired from the Boston Fire Department as a deputy chief.

James D. Gallagher

James D. Gallagher has quietly made a big difference in town. A cofounder, president and director of The One Fund Boston, Jim is also chairman of the Catholic Charities Boston Board of Trustees. He is executive vice president, general counsel, and chief administrative officer of John Hancock Financial. "My heritage has taught me to take nothing for granted, work hard, and take good care of my family, friends and colleagues," Jim says. Born the second child of "an energetic Irish family of seven" to Jim and Gertrude Gallagher in Detroit, Michigan, Jim counts his trips to Ireland among his favorite family memories. The most notable was in 2001 when Jim and his wife, Jo-Anne, their four children, and other family and friends toured the countryside. Among Jim's Irish antecedents are a paternal great-grandfather Patrick Gallagher, born in Co. Donegal, and a great-great-grandfather, Thomas Lavin, from Ballina, a town in north Co. Mayo.

Mayor Martin J. Walsh

That **Martin J. Walsh**'s campaign to be the 54th mayor of Boston grew from support in his Dorchester neighborhood to a broad coalition that included every part of the city was never more evident than on election night November 5, 2013, when the mayor-elect took the stage at the Park Plaza Hotel. "For this kid from Taft Street in Dorchester, you've made Boston a place where dreams come true," Walsh told his supporters. "Together, we're going to make Boston a place where dreams come true for every child, for every person, in every corner of this city." The son of Irish immigrants who was raised in a three-decker in the Savin Hill section of Dorchester, Marty became the first new mayor in 20 years. On stage with Marty, at left, is his longtime partner, Lorrie Higgins, her daughter, Lauren, and others who have supported him since he was first elected as state representative in 1997. He represented the 13th Suffolk District, where he was raised, for 16 years; it is one of the most diverse in the state.

Bryan Rafanelli

As the founder and chief creative officer of his eponymous events management firm, **Bryan Rafanelli** has overseen some of the biggest annual gatherings in Boston that have raised millions of dollars for area charities. His last name announces his Italian background, but he says his Irish heritage permeates his life. His family, the Ryans, came over from Co. Kerry in the 1920s. Bryan's great-grandfather John and his grandfather Frank were toolmakers. After coming through Ellis Island, they traveled to New England to settle with relatives. Bryan's great-uncle hit the road as a contractor helping to build bridges. Bryan credits that dedication with driving him to start up his business in the mid-1990s. He's not afraid to take on a challenge, as he did in 2014 when he ran the Boston Marathon to raise money for the MassGeneral Hospital for Children. Bryan's office overlooks the home stretch of the marathon route in the area that was racked by the bomb blasts the year before. Of his relatives, Bryan says, "They passed on their work ethic and dedication, and their strong features. I have been told I am the spitting image of my grandfather, who looked just like his father."

John Hailer

Growing up in Roslindale as one of 10 children, **John Hailer** learned early on that kindness and respect were two of the most important values, "because they were necessary for such a large family to function." John is the CEO of Natixis Global Asset Management for Asia and the Americas. Under his leadership, the firm has seen an impressive period of growth and is now recognized as one of the world's leading asset managers. He was photographed on the grounds of the Faulkner Hospital in Jamaica Plain where his mother, Mary, delivered her children. "In those days, kids weren't allowed in the hospital, so my mother would stand in the window with each new child. That's how we were introduced to the family," John says. His family traces its roots to Co. Cavan and Co. Tipperary. John's father, Frederick C. Hailer, Jr., was a Boston City Councilor for most of the 1950s. John is the chairman of the board of The New England Council and remains committed to local organizations, including The Home for Little Wanderers and the Irish International Immigration Center.

William W. Higgins, Jr. and William J. Higgins

It was while visiting Ireland in 1985 for the Shamrock Games that **William W. Higgins, Jr.** (left), shown with son **William J. Higgins**, was spurred into action and created the Southill Children's Fund, a Boston-based nonprofit that raises money to fund programs for children in Southill, Co. Limerick. Billy was traveling with Andrea, one of his four children, who, at 15, represented Boston in the games and stayed with a Southill family. "The similarities between the people there and my childhood experiences were very strong, and I felt this duty to do all I could for the children of Southill," says Billy, who was raised in South Boston. Since then, Billy, his wife, Rachel Cappuccio, and their family have led an all-volunteer team of fundraisers and sent thousands of dollars to support the Southill Junior School, the Holy Family parish's recreation and cultural programs, and an after-school boxing program. The fund has also paid for children from this parish on the south side of Limerick to travel to Boston and for Boston children to visit Ireland. Billy's son William, owner of William Higgins Insurance of South Boston, is continuing the fund. The family traces its Irish lineage back to Thomas Higgins of Co. Waterford, Billy's great-grandfather.

Stephen F. Lynch

U.S. Congressman **Stephen F. Lynch** represents the Eighth District of Massachusetts, which includes part of Boston, the cities of Brockton and Quincy, and towns throughout the South Shore of Massachusetts, which he proudly notes is known as "The Irish Riviera." The Congressman points out that his district also holds the title as having the most residents who claim Irish heritage. Steve's mother's family, the Havlins, came to the United States from Co. Kerry and the Lynches emigrated from Co. Galway in the early 19th

century. In 2012, Steve was elected to his seventh term in Congress, and he credits his Irish ancestors as a daily source of inspiration. Before his election to Congress, Steve was president of the Iron Workers Union, Local 7, and served in the Massachusetts House of Representatives and Massachusetts Senate. A lifelong resident of South Boston, Steve is a staple at the annual South Boston St. Patrick's Day Breakfast.

Doyle's Café

For more than 130 years, Doyle's Café on Washington Street has served as a meeting spot, a community bellwether, and the unofficial cornerstone of Jamaica Plain. For many years **Gerry Burke** (center) ran the pub and restaurant that *The Boston Globe*'s Brian Mooney described in 1996 thusly: "With lofty tin ceilings, walls adorned with murals, and precious Boston memorabilia, it's a favorite watering hole for powerful politicians and their coat-holders." In addition to political gatherings, Doyle's has hosted countless book parties and neighborhood celebrations. In 2005, his son **Gerry Burke** (left) and business partner **Christopher Spellman** took over the eatery that was once in the shadow of the MBTA's elevated Orange Line. The Burke family traces its roots back to the counties of Cork and Galway. When the elder Gerry, an astute student of Boston's Irish history and lore, speaks of his family, the stories are often filled with the heroes and rascals of the city's Irish past. One side of his family had the concessions at Franklin Park, and the other wing of his family ran the golf program. "The Burkes could sell you peanuts, and the Callahans could get you a tee time," Gerry says. He has been interviewed and featured in numerous media pieces on Boston and its Irish history, was part of the Disney-PBS series *The Irish in America*, and has lectured on the development of Washington Street for the Jamaica Plain Historical Society and others. The current ownership has made a few updates, but "kept Doyle's true to its Irish culture and charm."

Ronan Tynan

Raised on a dairy farm in Kilkenny, **Ronan Tynan**, Irish tenor, Paralympic athlete and physician, has sung for U.S. presidents and two popes. Ronan sang at the inauguration of George W. Bush, as a soloist at Ronald Reagan's funeral, and at the Vatican for Pope John Paul II and for Pope Benedict XVI. Ronan's connection to Boston was cemented in 2009 when he sang at the memorial service for U.S. Senator Edward M. Kennedy. The critically acclaimed tenor has performed at Boston's St. Patrick's Day Breakfast; from the fields of Gillette Stadium and Fenway Park; while rolling through the streets of Boston on a "Duck Boat" with the Red Sox following their 2013 World Series win; and at the inauguration of Boston Mayor Martin J. Walsh. Having been the voice of solace to many after 9/11, Ronan again stepped forward following the Boston Marathon bombings in 2013, singing at the funeral of Krystle Campbell, and, just about a year later, at the funerals of Lieutenant Edward J. Walsh, Jr. and Michael R. Kennedy, two Boston firefighters who were killed in a Back Bay blaze. In 2014, Ronan achieved another long-awaited goal: the arrival of his green card. Of this, he said simply: "Always Irish, but now, too, American."

John Joseph Moakley

Congressman **John Joseph Moakley** was a powerful figure in Washington, D.C., and even more so in Boston, but he wasn't a man of pretense. *The New York Times* said that "for a half-century [Joe] was the proud quintessence of the South Boston Irish Democrat," and there wasn't anything within his abilities that he would deny a constituent. When he died on May 29, 2001, thousands turned out at the State House to pay their respects. Hundreds also lined the route—sometimes four deep—that his funeral cortege followed as it made its way from St. Brigid Church on East Broadway in South Boston. Among the many to attend the funeral Mass were President George W. Bush, former President Bill Clinton, and Joe's longtime political ally Al Gore. It was fitting that political foes would gather to pay their respects to Joe, who was known for working with the other side of the aisle in his 30-year career in the U.S. House of Representatives.

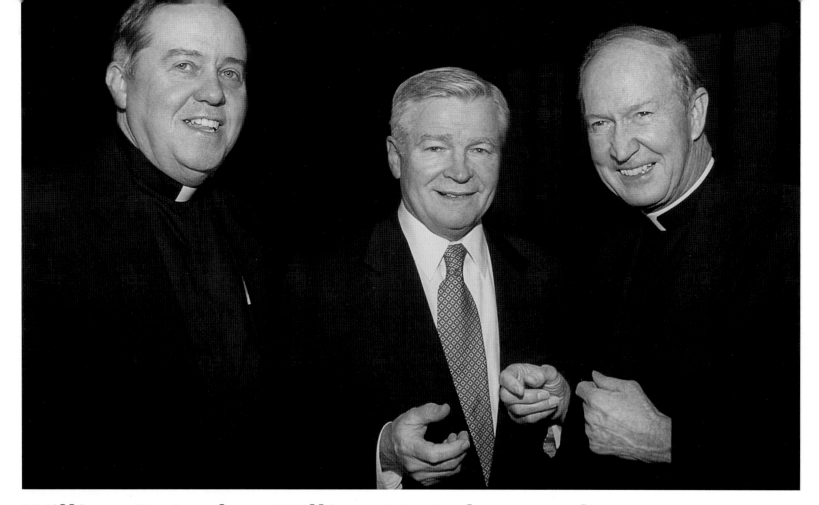

William P. Leahy, William M. Bulger, and J. Donald Monan

The presidencies of Reverend **William P. Leahy**, SJ, (left) and Reverend **J. Donald Monan**, SJ, span 42 years in the life of Boston College, which was founded in the South End in 1863 by the Society of Jesus as an avenue to higher education for the sons of Irish immigrants. The two were photographed with **William M. Bulger** (center), a Triple Eagle: He graduated from Boston College High School in 1952, then enrolled at Boston College, leaving after a year for a stint in the U.S. Army. He returned in 1955, earning his degree three years later, after which he received his degree from Boston College Law School in 1961. He was awarded an honorary Doctor of Laws degree by the National University of Ireland, Galway in 2002. The Bulgers emigrated from New Ross, Co. Wexford, and William's mother's family—the McCarthys—hailed from Cork City. The Bulgers lived for a time on Carson Street in Dorchester, and, when William was four years old, they were one of the first families to move to Old Harbor Village in South Boston. William served in the Legislature for more than 35 years and was president of the University of Massachusetts from 1996 until 2003. A third-generation Irish American whose family came from Co. Kerry, Father Leahy grew up on an Iowa corn farm and set his sights on becoming a scholar on 20th-century American social and religious history. Named the college's 25th president in 1996, he has led the university's continuing rise to the upper echelon of American higher education. Father Monan, who has family roots in Northern Ireland, now serves as university chancellor at Boston College. During a 24-year presidency that began in 1972, Father Monan led the college from its commuter-student days to national prominence. He was awarded an honorary degree by the National University of Ireland.

John Paul Patrick Walsh

Self-made businessman **John Paul Patrick Walsh** has chalked up a notable number of successes in real estate, finance, beauty care, and film. John attributes his entrepreneurial acumen to the "advanced degree in business I received as a resident of the Somerville housing projects." John was photographed outside the Algonquin Club, a private social club in the Back Bay for business leaders, where he is a member. A dual citizen of Ireland and the United States, John is a second-generation Irish American who traces his ancestry to the rugged Gaelic-speaking terrain of Oughterard, Co. Galway. His company Elizabeth Grady, a skin-care salon company with 30 locations and thriving schools, has sponsored many charities. Both John, who is a member of the Ancient Order of Hibernians, and his company have received numerous awards for social responsibility. John says, "My family and I were born wealthy and money had nothing to do with it."

Kevin Cullen and Shelley Murphy

Friends and colleagues at *The Boston Globe*, **Kevin Cullen** and **Shelley Murphy** are considered to be among the city's best journalists. They cowrote the 2013 *New York Times* best seller *Whitey Bulger, America's Most Wanted Gangster and the Manhunt That Brought Him to Justice* and were contributors to the newspaper's Pulitzer Prize-winning coverage of the Boston Marathon bombings. Kevin, a metro section columnist, has written for *The Globe* since 1985. He is the grandson of immigrants from Connemara and carries an Irish passport, which has saved him abroad on more than one occasion. His enrollment at Trinity College in Dublin, in 1979, led to a continuing professional interest in Ireland. He covered the conflict in Northern Ireland for many years and in 1997 was appointed *The Globe*'s Dublin bureau chief. *The Irish Times* has called him "the most informed American journalist on Irish affairs." Though he moved to London for a stint as a European correspondent, in 2001, he returned to Boston to join *The Globe*'s Pulitzer Prize-winning investigative team that exposed the cover-up of sexual abuse by Catholic priests. Shelley's paternal grandparents, Bridget Nagle and Eugene Murphy, emigrated from Co. Kerry to Boston during the early 20th century and settled in the Savin Hill neighborhood of Dorchester. After graduating from college, she and a cousin backpacked through Ireland and found relatives near Killarney who shared photos of their grandfather as a young man. Shelley has covered organized crime in Boston since the early 1980s, writing extensively about the notorious Irish gangster James "Whitey" Bulger and his rivals in the city's mob scene.

Patricia Queeney

Patricia Queeney turned her 30-year career as a hairdresser and makeup artist into a business that helps people undergoing chemotherapy and radiation treatment feel better about facing the world. Owner of Patricia and Company, she first started working with oncology patients who wanted to get a wig specifically styled, fitted, and tailored. The South Shore company's services expanded to include specialty clothing, instruction on how to apply makeup, and other problems facing those with cancer.

Patricia grew up in Dorchester "in St. Brendan's Parish…you must specify the parish or you truly are not from Boston," she says. Her father, Arthur Queeney, traces his family roots from Co. Cork, and his family settled in Roxbury. Both of Patricia's grandfathers and her father were Boston Police officers. Grandfather Murphy walked the beat in Charlestown and Arthur patrolled Mattapan Square. Now, two of Patricia's three sons are Boston firefighters.

Gregory E. Bulger

After watching students at Boston College High School give a performance in a converted lab one night, alumnus **Gregory E. Bulger** was moved to help the school's drama department. The Gregory E. Bulger Performing Arts Center, which opened in 2007, is a state-of-the-art, 351-seat performance space located at the site that was once occupied by the Dever Gym and Auditorium. Part of a large Irish-Catholic family from St. Columbkille's Parish in Brighton, Greg attended Boston College High and then Boston College. He began his career at the Mattapan Community Health Center and later founded HealthCare Value Management. After selling his company, Greg started a foundation that now supports performing arts and cultural organizations. Well known in Boston's classical music community, Greg is an overseer of the Boston Symphony Orchestra and supports the Boston Early Music Festival. In 2013, Boston College High School enlisted Greg's help for its sold-out 150th anniversary celebration at Boston Symphony Hall.

Celia McDonough

The calm scenes of **Celia McDonough**'s watercolors have become familiar to many Dorchester residents and expatriates. Now the Neponset resident's paintings, featured in an annual calendar, have caught on beyond the city's largest neighborhood. Celia is a watercolorist who also works full-time as assistant to Mark Erlich, executive secretary-treasurer of the New England Regional Council of Carpenters. Celia and her husband, John, have been married for 50 years and have five children and 12 grandchildren. Like many Irish families that came to the Boston area in the mid-19th century, Celia and her husband's ancestors left Ireland to escape the harsh conditions and poverty that crippled the country. Celia's maternal grandparents were from Co. Roscommon and Co. Clare and settled in Dorchester before moving to Roxbury. Her paternal grandparents were second-generation Irish American. Celia's grandmother Anastasia was raised in the North End, and her grandfather Frederick's family came from Nova Scotia to Hyde Park, where the couple lived and raised 10 children.

Sean and Gerry Morrissey

Sean Morrissey (left) and **Gerry Morrissey** learned of their Irish heritage at an early age. Their maternal grandfather, Patrick J. Walsh, would often bewilder the kids with his recitation of Gaelic, although there was no one in the house to authenticate his verse. The men say their mother, Eleanor (Walsh) Morrissey, who died in August 2014, loved all things Irish—particularly Joyce, Yeats, and Heaney—and passed that on to them as well. Like so many Irish-Americans, the brothers were drawn to politics and public service. Gerry has served in the administrations of six consecutive governors, advocating on behalf of individuals with intellectual and developmental disabilities. He is considered a national thought leader on mental health and disability issues and serves as the chief quality officer of The MENTOR Network. Principal of Morrissey & Associates, a Boston-based consulting firm, Sean spent more than two decades as a member of leadership staff in the Massachusetts House of Representatives. The brothers are engaged in local community, fraternal, and philanthropic organizations and serve on a number of nonprofit boards including the Boys & Girls Clubs of Dorchester, Massachusetts Association of Mental Health, New England Center for Children, Special Olympics of Massachusetts, Community Resources for Justice, Best Buddies International, and The Arc of Massachusetts.

Brigadier General Jack Hammond

Like many of Boston's Irish-Americans, **Jack Hammond** chose a career in the military. Jack rose to the rank of Brigadier General, commanding troops in both Iraq and Afghanistan. He retired from the Army after returning home from Afghanistan in 2012 and now works for the Red Sox and Massachusetts General Hospital. He leads the Home Base Program, which operates the only private sector clinic in America focused solely on healing the invisible wounds of war. "We now lose 22 veterans a day to suicide," says Jack.

"Our Iraq and Afghanistan Veterans and their families need our help." He draws strength from his heritage—all four of Jack's grandparents were 100-percent Irish—and says his ancestors were great role models. Jack's grandfather emigrated from Co. Louth as a servant, lost his arm working for the railroad, and later graduated from Northeastern University's School of Law in 1912. He became the city attorney for Cambridge "and helped get Tip O'Neill elected to the Massachusetts Legislature."

Robert Haley

When **Robert Haley** was recognized by the government of France and presented with the Chevalier Legion of Honor medallion at a ceremony in 2103 at Weymouth town hall, the 90-year-old World War II veteran insisted he wasn't a hero. But others tell a different story: one of heroism and bravery during the D-Day invasion of Omaha Beach on the Normandy Coast. Bob is the oldest of three sons born to Egbert Thomas Haley and Catherine Ahearn on May 17,1923, at St. Margaret's Hospital in Boston. Bob is of 100-percent Irish descent, as are the three generations that succeeded him. Bob's mother's family emigrated from Co. Down to Canada and made their way to Boston. Bob's father's family emigrated from West Meath to Boston. He enlisted in the U.S. Navy in 1942—his brothers William and James also served in World War II. Following the war, he married Mary Hogan, whose family came from Co. Tipperary, and embarked on a 45-year career as a sales engineer with the National Research Corporation, later working in the Veteran's Services office in Weymouth.

Brendan and Greg Feeney

The trucks and crews from Feeney Brothers Excavation are ubiquitous in parts of the Northeast, but it all started with **Brendan Feeney** (left) who worked in landscaping and construction in the early 1980s. When his brother Greg followed him to Boston from their native Enniscrone, Co. Sligo, they started their own business with the purchase of a single backhoe in 1986. "We worked around the clock back in the '80s," **Greg** told the *Dorchester Reporter*. Nearly 30 years later, Feeney Brothers Excavation has more than 400 employees throughout Massachusetts, Connecticut, and New York and is a leading utility contractor. The company, run out of Dorchester headquarters, has done projects at Logan International Airport and Fenway Park. Both brothers trained as engineers back in their native Sligo and have been involved in their industry's trade associations, working on training and safety. They also support a number of charities and have been recognized by the *Boston Irish Reporter* for their service to the community.

Joyce Linehan

"I'm a convener by nature," **Joyce Linehan** told a *Boston Globe* reporter in 2005. Indeed, this music publicist, arts advocate, and political activist, now Chief of Policy for Mayor Walsh, is known for bringing different groups of people together. Joyce's home in Dorchester's Lower Mills, where this photograph was taken, has been dubbed "Ashmonticello" by friends and gained a reputation as a gathering place for organizers and policy wonks. Her living room has been the launching pad for several campaigns, including two notable successes: Elizabeth Warren's run for U.S. Senate and Martin J. Walsh's bid for Mayor of Boston. A Dorchester native, Joyce's father, John J.

Linehan, a first generation Irish-American with roots in Macroom, Co. Cork, was a state representative from Mission Hill in the late 1950s, after winning the seat his father held. By the time Joyce entered the political fray she already had a successful career as a music manager and publicist and co-owner of the Ashmont Records label. Among the bands Joyce managed are The Smithereens and The Lemonheads. And, for most of the 1990s, she ran the East Coast operation of Sub Pop Records, which launched the careers of Nirvana, The Afghan Whigs, and Sebadoh, among others.

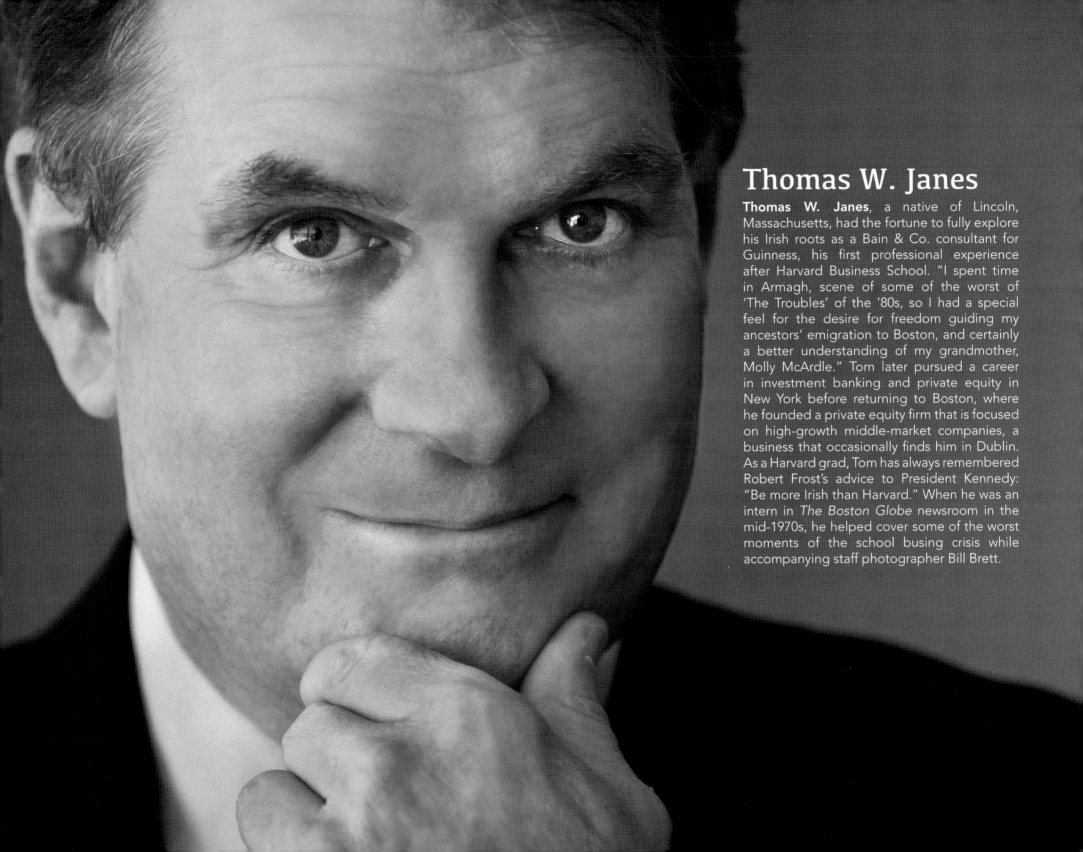

Thomas W. Janes

Thomas W. Janes, a native of Lincoln, Massachusetts, had the fortune to fully explore his Irish roots as a Bain & Co. consultant for Guinness, his first professional experience after Harvard Business School. "I spent time in Armagh, scene of some of the worst of 'The Troubles' of the '80s, so I had a special feel for the desire for freedom guiding my ancestors' emigration to Boston, and certainly a better understanding of my grandmother, Molly McArdle." Tom later pursued a career in investment banking and private equity in New York before returning to Boston, where he founded a private equity firm that is focused on high-growth middle-market companies, a business that occasionally finds him in Dublin. As a Harvard grad, Tom has always remembered Robert Frost's advice to President Kennedy: "Be more Irish than Harvard." When he was an intern in *The Boston Globe* newsroom in the mid-1970s, he helped cover some of the worst moments of the school busing crisis while accompanying staff photographer Bill Brett.

Ted Oatis

Up until shortly before his death on August 21, 2014, at age 67, **Ted Oatis** would spend part of each day walking around International Place—the downtown towers that he developed with business partner Don Chiofaro that changed Boston's skyline. Ted and Don started the Chiofaro Company in 1980, and their projects included New England Biolabs, Westborough Technology Park, and the Boston Harbor Garage. The Oatis family left Ireland in 1850 with a number of adult children, and settled in Toledo, Ohio, where Theodore Allen Oatis was born to Richard and Ruth (Taylor) Oatis. The family ran the Oatis Machinery Company. Ted attended Brown University and, later, Harvard Business School. A father of three, Ted raised his children after his first wife, Elizabeth, died of complications from melanoma at age 40 in 1990. "He knew he had his work cut out for him, but I never heard him say, 'Poor me.' He never quit," his business partner told *The Boston Globe*. Shortly after his death, they dimmed the lights of International Place in Ted's honor.

Maureen E. Feeney, Michael F. Flaherty and Stephen J. Murphy

For his January 6, 2014, inauguration as Boston's 54th mayor, **Martin J. Walsh** called upon **Yo-Yo Ma** to play during the ceremony at Boston College's Conte Forum. The famed cellist, who calls Cambridge home, artfully managed to play *Danny Boy* between more classical selections. City Clerk **Maureen E. Feeney**, and City Councilors **Michael F. Flaherty** and **Stephen J. Murphy** (right) are shown on stage listening to the performance. All three city officials have served as City Council president. Maureen represented Dorchester on the City Council from 1994 to 2011, when she resigned from office and was subsequently appointed clerk. She was council president for one term. Her family's roots are in Cahersiveen in Co. Kerry and Skibbereen in Co. Cork. Although she entered politics later than some, Maureen says that her family was always politically active. The first wake she attended was for James Michael Curley. The Flaherty's story starts in Co. Galway's Connemara region with forebears from Camus, Lettermore, and Rosmuc, and continues in South Boston, where they settled and where Mike was born and raised. He served as a city councilor from 2000 to 2010, when he unsuccessfully challenged Mayor Menino. He was council president from 2002 to 2006 and regained a seat on the council in the 2013 election. His father, Michael, is a former state representative and former associate justice on the Boston Municipal Court. The Murphy story in America begins in 1848 with the family settling in East Boston. Steve counts police officers and a baker who helped create the famed Parker House rolls among his ancestors. From East Boston, Steve's family moved to Charlestown, Roxbury, Dorchester, and Hyde Park, where he now lives. "We traveled 14 miles in 170 years," Steve says. He has been on the city council since 1997 and served three terms as council president. Steve graduated from Boston Latin as part of the last all-male class.

The O'Neill Family

Sara and **Diarmuid O'Neill** believe that America really is the land of opportunity. "When you arrive here, the first thing you realize is just how positive people are. Americans believe anything is possible and now so do I," says Diarmuid, who emigrated from Cork City in the mid-1980s and landed a job at J.J. Foley's on Kingston Street. Sara arrived a few years later from "Derry City in the North of Ireland" and was hired at The Littlest Bar then located on Province Street in Downtown Crossing. Diarmuid and Sara opened The Squealing Pig in the former Chandler's space in Mission Hill in the late 1990s, and they now own The Squealing Pig in Provincetown, Tavern at the End of the World in Charlestown and others. A few years ago, the couple looked to adopt children from Ethiopia, learned of two siblings who needed a home, and ultimately discovered that four young siblings might be split up—so they adopted all four. The children, photographed with their parents, are, from left: **Rahel**, 7; **Bezawit**, 10; **Selamawit**, 8; "and, finally, our wee boy is **Andualem**, and he is five," the proud mother says. All four are enrolled in St. Mary of the Assumption Elementary School in Brookline. Sara and Diarmuid took their children on their first trip to Ireland in the summer of 2014, where they toured the Antrim coast, and "they just had a blast. In fact, they all want to move there," says Sara. Previously, the family traveled to Africa. "I want them to not just know who they are, but know—remember— where they came from," Diarmuid says.

Paul G. Kirk, Jr.

Paul G. Kirk, Jr. served as a U.S. Senator, representing Massachusetts from September 2009 until February 2010, and filling the vacancy left by Edward M. Kennedy's death. Chairman of Kirk & Associates, Inc., Paul, was a founding director of the John F. Kennedy Library Foundation, serving as its chairman from 1992 to 2009. He is also a founding director of the Dorchester-based Edward M. Kennedy Institute for the United States Senate and served as chairman of the National Democratic Party and founding cochairman of the Commission on Presidential Debates. A graduate of Harvard College and Harvard Law School, Paul was a partner in the law firm of Sullivan & Worcester of Boston. His grandfather, John Lennon Kirk, was born in Co. Louth and settled in East Boston, where he and his wife, Maud, raised 14 children, including Paul's late father, Supreme Judicial Court Justice Paul Grattan Kirk, who served as a Colonel in the U.S. Army's 26th "Yankee" Division during World War II. Paul's mother, Josephine O'Connell, traced her heritage to Co. Cavan. Her uncle was William Henry O'Connell, the first Cardinal Archbishop of Boston.

John White

John White, managing director and head of capital markets, Boston, at Barclays, says that his grandparents—Nora and John J. White from Co. Cork—were his role models growing up in the city. "They worked hard, and they always had their door open for me," he says. John, the oldest of seven, says that because he spent so much time with his grandparents, he claims two Boston neighborhoods (Jamaica Plain and Mission Hill) and attended Mass in two parishes (Blessed Sacrament in Jamaica Plain and St. Patrick's in Roxbury). A graduate of Tabor Academy, John graduated from Tufts University and the Fletcher School of Law and Diplomacy. While at Tufts, he played basketball and was the cocaptain of the squad. He later coached for a few years, and one of his players was former Massachusetts Senator Scott Brown. The lessons of his childhood push him to support charitable work that helps inner-city youth, including the POSSE Foundation, which provides scholarships and support for students with leadership potential.

Kenneth K. Quigley, Jr.

Kenneth K. Quigley, Jr.'s family tradition of education extends to Ireland. Ken, the fourteenth president of Curry College in Milton, Massachusetts, was born in Dublin and holds dual U.S. and Irish citizenship. His son Kevin studied abroad his junior year at National University Ireland, Maynooth, and Ken's father, Kenneth Sr., was a physician who earned his degree at the University College of Dublin School of Medicine. In this photograph, Ken is shown in front of the 84,000-square-foot Curry College Student Center, one of the many new facilities on the campus since Ken's tenure began in 1996. Those new dormitories and classroom buildings were needed to accommodate the tripling of the student enrollment and the new undergraduate and graduate degree programs added during Ken's presidency. In addition to his work at Curry, Ken supports a number of professional, civic and charitable organizations, including The New England Council and The Rodman Ride for Kids, Inc.

David Doyle and Michael Feighery

Both **David Doyle** (left) and **Michael Feighery** come from families with traditions in the hospitality industry. The two led the team that opened the Smith & Wollensky steakhouse on Atlantic Wharf. Born, raised, and educated in Ireland, David first worked for his parents, Tom and Mary, owners of Tommy Doyle's pub in Baltinglass, Co. Wicklow, which has been in the Doyle family since 1886, serving locals, tourists, and celebrities from near and far. He moved to the United States in 1992, worked for the Hilton Hotels in Chicago and first joined Smith & Wollensky as a floor manager in Chicago. He was employed by the premium steak restaurant company as general manager in Las Vegas, Washington, D.C., and then in Boston. A 29-year veteran of Smith & Wollensky, Michael joined the company in

1986 as a butcher's assistant and now leads the Boston-based Smith & Wollensky Restaurant Group as president and CEO. Michael's Dublin-born parents, Olive and Tom, ran a modest pub in Burnt Oak, an Irish area of North London. He eventually became chef at the famed Rosleague Manor in Connemara. In 1976, with little more than $400 in his pocket and the address of a distant relative living in New York, Michael came to America and landed an entry-level job in the kitchen of the Smith & Wollensky restaurant in Manhattan. He quickly earned promotions to kitchen manager, chef, floor manager, and to running the Boston-based company. Michael is involved in fundraising with the Keep Memory Alive program at the Cleveland Clinic Lou Ruvo Center for Brain Health.

Jack Doherty

Jack Doherty's bucket list includes a trip to the Emerald Isle, but the rigors of running College Hype, his Dorchester-based apparel company, have kept him closer to home, he says. And yet, this father of five is bringing Ireland a little closer to Boston and to the many people who, like Jack, have strong Irish roots. Jack's company has created more than 50 unique Irish T-shirts through their Irish Hype label and website. (www.IrishHype.com) Mayor Walsh and Mark Wahlberg are two of the many famous Bostonians who have been spotted in College Hype and Irish Hype gear. Eagle-eyed film aficionados may have seen the apparel worn in movies filmed locally, including *The Town* and *Gone Baby Gone*. Jack's great-grandparents John J. Doherty and Mary Lorden hailed from Co. Cork and Co. Kerry, and his maternal grandparents called Co. Waterford home. "Ireland is a big part of our family heritage," Jack says, "and what better place to be Irish than in Boston."

Dan Rea

It is said that the Irish have the "gift of gab," and since 2007 **Dan Rea** has utilized his gift as the host of WBZ NewsRadio 1030's issues talk show *NightSide*, which airs weeknights from 8 to midnight on New England's first radio station. Dan traces his roots to the Co. Cork town of Mallow, on the Blackwater River, where Dan's cousins still live. During the 1980s and into the 1990s, Dan reported from the Republic and Northern Ireland for WBZ-TV on the economic and social troubles that plagued the land of his father's parents and his mother's grandparents. Dan graduated from St. Anne's School in Readville, Boston Latin School, Boston State College, and earned his law degree from Boston University Law School. The recipient of three honorary doctorates, Dan was also awarded the Silver Shingle from Boston University Law School, Regional Emmys, and the Yankee Quill award, the region's most significant individual journalism honor.

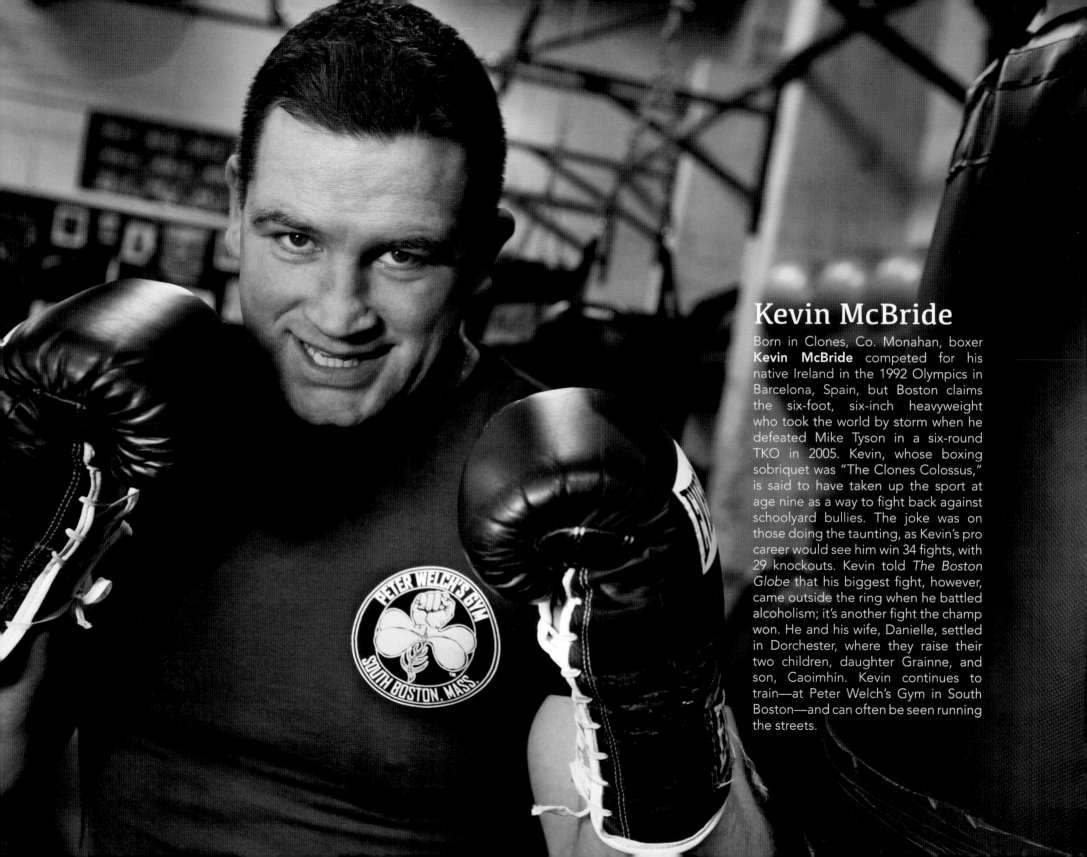

Kevin McBride

Born in Clones, Co. Monahan, boxer **Kevin McBride** competed for his native Ireland in the 1992 Olympics in Barcelona, Spain, but Boston claims the six-foot, six-inch heavyweight who took the world by storm when he defeated Mike Tyson in a six-round TKO in 2005. Kevin, whose boxing sobriquet was "The Clones Colossus," is said to have taken up the sport at age nine as a way to fight back against schoolyard bullies. The joke was on those doing the taunting, as Kevin's pro career would see him win 34 fights, with 29 knockouts. Kevin told *The Boston Globe* that his biggest fight, however, came outside the ring when he battled alcoholism; it's another fight the champ won. He and his wife, Danielle, settled in Dorchester, where they raise their two children, daughter Grainne, and son, Caoimhín. Kevin continues to train—at Peter Welch's Gym in South Boston—and can often be seen running the streets.

The Leary Family

Two brothers and two of their sons, all part of the large Leary family of Boston, are "100-percent Irish-American," tracing their heritage to the counties of Cork and Wexford. Daniel Leary and his wife, Margaret, emigrated from the West Cork village of Inchigeela and settled in South Boston. The fathers remember their own grandfathers, Michael J. Leary, a Boston firefighter, and Dr. William F. Nolan, one of the city's first Irish physicians. **Joseph F. Leary, Jr**. (left) worked for the Gillette Company for 30 years in various positions and is now president and CEO of the Irish American Partnership, a national charity that specializes in assisting Irish education in both the north and south of Ireland. More than 500 Irish schools have received grants from the Partnership. His son

Joseph F. Leary III owns his own real estate business in Boston with a focus on serving small businesses. **Kevin W. Leary** (third from left) founded VPNE Parking Solutions in 1990. His vision, as a former U.S. Naval Officer and 25-year veteran of the investment banking industry, was for the parking experience to be one of the highlights of the visit, similar to the experience in the lobby of a hotel, hospital, office building or executive suite. In 1992, he encouraged his son **Kevin J. Leary** (far right) to join the firm after receiving his degree from Villanova University. Today, VPNE provides parking, staffing, and shuttle services to more than 100 of New England's healthcare, hotel, and commercial real estate companies.

Maura S. Doyle

When **Maura S. Doyle** was sworn in on October 21, 1996, as clerk of the Supreme Judicial Court for Suffolk County, she became the first woman to hold the position since its inception in 1693. Among her many duties, Maura conducts the twice-annual admission ceremony at which each new class of attorneys is admitted to the Massachusetts Bar. Maura is shown here presiding over the swearing in ceremony in June 2014 and estimates that she has sworn in more than 36,000 attorneys in nearly 20 years in office. Also on stage, at left, is Massachusetts Supreme Judicial Court Chief Justice **Ralph D. Gants**, then an associate justice who participated in the ceremony. A Boston native, Maura received a bachelor's degree in criminal justice from Northeastern University and her law degree from Suffolk University School of Law. Maura and her husband, attorney Frank Doyle, have three children and live in Dorchester—St. Brendan's Parish—where they are involved in a number of community and civic organizations. Her family traces its roots to Co. Cork, including one branch of the family that made its way to Boston via Nova Scotia.

Diane M. Sullivan

Diane M. Sullivan, professor of law and assistant dean of students at the Massachusetts School of Law, is a longtime animal advocate. The first of her family to go to college, she lists her greatest professional accomplishments as the creation of the school's animal law program and the nonprofit charity, The Shadow Fund, which was established to help indigent pet owners with funding for medical expenses for beloved pets. She also is host and producer of the award-winning regional television show *The Educational Forum*. Diane's steadfast loyalty to a cause is something she traces to her grandparents who left Ireland for the west side of Fitchburg, then the city's Irish side. "In my house, few things mattered more than Notre Dame football," Diane says. "When the 'Irish' lost a Saturday afternoon game, my grandfather refused to eat and went straight to bed at four o'clock in the afternoon." In fact, her father was named after Jack Elder, a key player on Knute Rockne's championship team.

Mary Kakas

"People assume I'm all sorts of nationalities, but really, I'm an Irish gal from South Boston," says **Mary Kakas**. Born at the former Carney Hospital (now Marian Manor) to Martin J. and Catherine (Carr) Walsh, Mary was raised in St. Brigid's Parish in South Boston. She jokes about a discussion with Boston's mayor. "He's Martin J. Walsh and his mother is Mary Joan Walsh, the same as my name on my birth certificate. My parents both came from Galway…so we think our families must be related." Her parents honored their heritage and

gave their children every chance to succeed. "My father had a heavy brogue, but my mother had an accent," Mary says. Anxious that his daughter "not be seen as some Irish country girl," her father sent her to elocution lessons. Mary lost all traces of Ireland and South Boston in her speech and put that to use when she managed Kakas Furs on Newbury Street, which closed in 2000 after 146 years of business. She now devotes her time to 10 charities and says, "I want to support those groups where my work can make a difference."

Paul J. McNamara

Paul J. McNamara considers himself lucky to have been born in Boston to Irish-American parents. Growing up in Jamaica Plain, attending St. Thomas Aquinas grammar school, and becoming a "Triple Eagle" (graduating from Boston College High School, Boston College and Boston College Law School), have allowed Paul a front-row seat to Boston's Irish-American community and its culture. Paul says that he and his two brothers inherited their ancestors' beliefs in giving back to their community. He served as president of the Charitable Irish Society of Boston, which was established in 1737 and is the oldest Irish society in the Americas. Paul also has served as president of the Catholic Lawyers Guild of Boston and as a member of the board of Catholic Charities Archdiocese of Boston. In his professional life, Paul says he has found great reward in representing institutional investors in the creation of housing developments for low- and moderate-income families in the South End, Roxbury, and Dorchester.

Kevin Doherty

That's 19-year-old fiddler **Kevin Doherty** of Dorchester atop a backhoe from the family business, K. Doherty Construction, during a break in his day. "I carry the fiddle with me almost all the time," Kevin says. "But I don't normally play *at* work." He did give an impromptu concert for this photograph, taken in a parking area at Pope John Paul II Park in Dorchester. Kevin keeps a pretty busy schedule. By day he works with his father, also Kevin, on construction sites and, afterwards, attends the construction management night program at Wentworth Institute of Technology. This branch of the Dohertys is from Donegal, a place Kevin visits twice a year. He performs with area bands and is a regular at the Cape Cod Irish Village in Yarmouth. "I just tell people that I'm a construction worker on weekdays," says Kevin, "and a fiddler on the weekends."

Anne Finucane and Mike Barnicle

Anne Finucane and **Mike Barnicle** are one of Boston's leading couples and both are proud of their Irish heritage. For many years, Mike has reported on the Irish—in Boston, New York and in Ireland itself. He has been recognized for his work from Northern Ireland to Co. Cork in his commentaries and columns for WCVB-TV, ABC News' *Nightline*, *The Boston Globe* and the *Daily News* in New York. Anne is Bank of America's Global Chief Strategy and Marketing Officer and president of the bank's Northeast region. She has combined her professional and personal interests in Ireland as a longtime board member of the American Ireland Fund and the Taoiseach's Economic Advisory Board. As the chairwoman of the Bank of America's foundation, Anne has spearheaded the bank's work with Bono, singer and front man of the band U2, on his efforts fighting mother-to-child transmission of HIV/Aids in Africa. Both Anne and Mike are of 100-percent Irish descent. Mike's family is from Mayo and Sligo, while Anne's hails from Cork and Kerry.

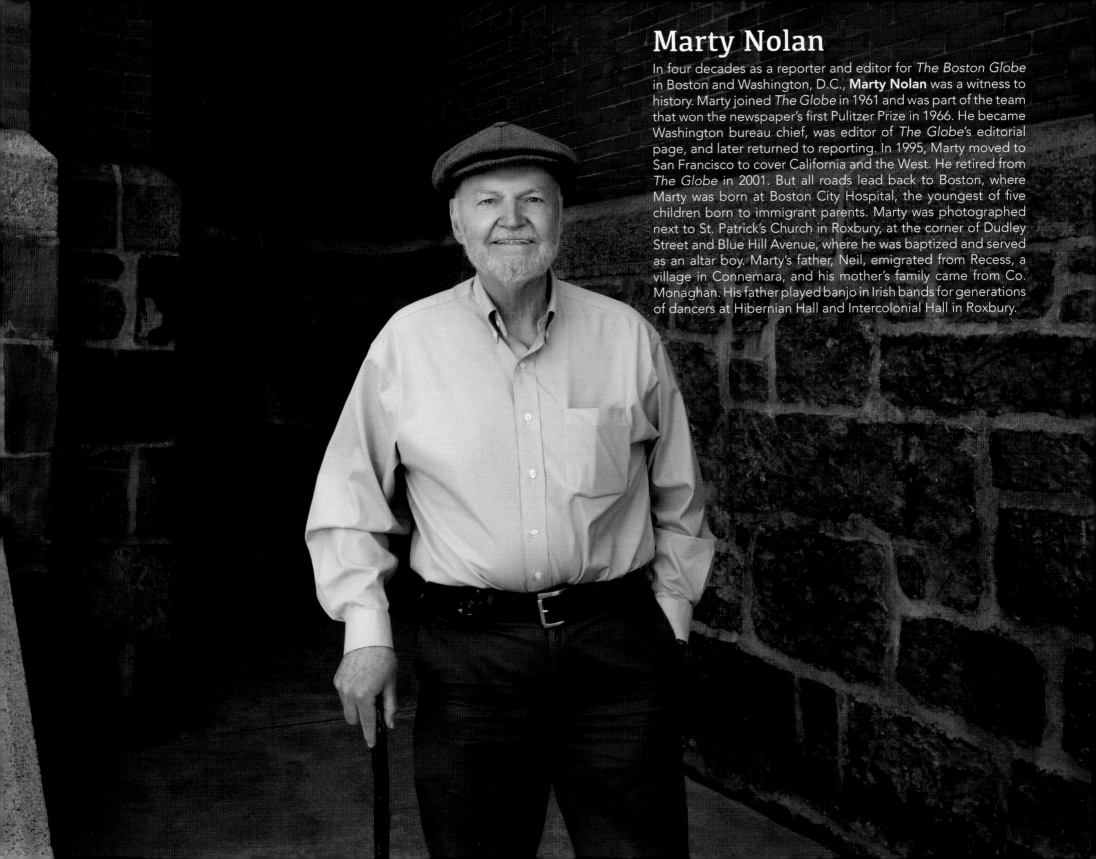

Marty Nolan

In four decades as a reporter and editor for *The Boston Globe* in Boston and Washington, D.C., **Marty Nolan** was a witness to history. Marty joined *The Globe* in 1961 and was part of the team that won the newspaper's first Pulitzer Prize in 1966. He became Washington bureau chief, was editor of *The Globe*'s editorial page, and later returned to reporting. In 1995, Marty moved to San Francisco to cover California and the West. He retired from *The Globe* in 2001. But all roads lead back to Boston, where Marty was born at Boston City Hospital, the youngest of five children born to immigrant parents. Marty was photographed next to St. Patrick's Church in Roxbury, at the corner of Dudley Street and Blue Hill Avenue, where he was baptized and served as an altar boy. Marty's father, Neil, emigrated from Recess, a village in Connemara, and his mother's family came from Co. Monaghan. His father played banjo in Irish bands for generations of dancers at Hibernian Hall and Intercolonial Hall in Roxbury.

Sister Evelyn Hurley

The first thing Bill Brett noticed about **Sister Evelyn Hurley**, SCN, who was walking in South Boston, was her coat. Sister Evelyn recounted how she knitted it herself. She created countless sweaters and blankets for families in South Boston, where she worked for many years as a teacher and principal at St. Brigid and the former Nazareth School. Sister Evelyn celebrated her 99th birthday on March 7, 2014, and marked her 80th anniversary of entering the order of the Sisters of Nazareth a few weeks later. She was the last member of her community to live in South Boston, where the sisters' first convent was built at the corner of M Street and East Broadway more than a century ago. Fittingly, the South Boston community held a "time" for Sister Evelyn, but it was a bittersweet day as her order decided to close the convent and have Sister Evelyn, who stopped teaching in 1995, officially retire to Kentucky. Boston City Councilor Michael Flaherty brought his former teacher to City Hall where he and his colleagues recognized her by naming her birthday as Sister Evelyn Hurley Day in the city. It was an appropriate tribute for Sister Evelyn, whose father, Bill Hurley, was a Boston City Councilor for 20 years who later opened Billy Hurley's Log Cabin, a restaurant and political hot spot for years.

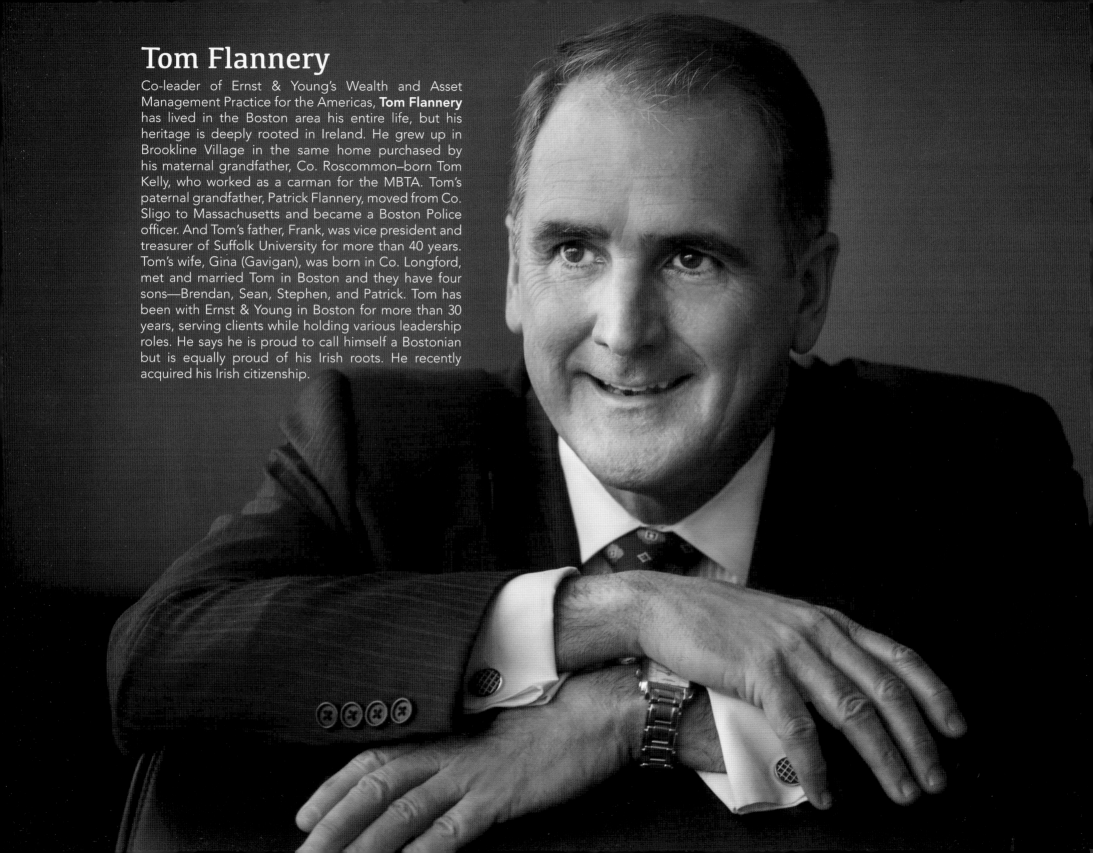

Tom Flannery

Co-leader of Ernst & Young's Wealth and Asset Management Practice for the Americas, **Tom Flannery** has lived in the Boston area his entire life, but his heritage is deeply rooted in Ireland. He grew up in Brookline Village in the same home purchased by his maternal grandfather, Co. Roscommon–born Tom Kelly, who worked as a carman for the MBTA. Tom's paternal grandfather, Patrick Flannery, moved from Co. Sligo to Massachusetts and became a Boston Police officer. And Tom's father, Frank, was vice president and treasurer of Suffolk University for more than 40 years. Tom's wife, Gina (Gavigan), was born in Co. Longford, met and married Tom in Boston and they have four sons—Brendan, Sean, Stephen, and Patrick. Tom has been with Ernst & Young in Boston for more than 30 years, serving clients while holding various leadership roles. He says he is proud to call himself a Bostonian but is equally proud of his Irish roots. He recently acquired his Irish citizenship.

George K. Regan, Jr.

Embodying the stamina of his working-class father, Boston public relations maestro **George K. Regan, Jr.**, was born to Irish-American George Sr., a South Boston native and veteran of both the Navy and Charlestown shipyards, and Ann (Kowalski). George's paternal grandfather was born in Co. Cork and came to Boston in the early 20th century. After graduating from North Quincy High School, George received his diploma from Suffolk University as a journalism major, and earned a master's degree in communication from Boston University. In his late teens, Regan worked as an ad messenger and copy boy for *The Boston Globe*. He eventually rose to become the right-hand man to a member of Boston's political—and Irish—elite, Mayor Kevin White. As press secretary, director of communications and spokesman, George provided counsel to White throughout his 16 years in office, particularly during Boston's turbulent busing crisis. Today, George remains

Bill McNally

Bill McNally served as the first executive director of the American Ireland Fund from 1982 to 1993. He played a central role in the early and substantial growth of the Fund as he planned and executed its fundraising strategies and programs to fulfill its mission of promoting peace, culture, and charity for the people of Ireland, North and South. He and his wife, Anne, traveled often to Ireland and Northern Ireland in the 1980s to encourage the development of peace and reconciliation programs and other social initiatives throughout the island. He continues to serve as legal counsel to the organization and as a member of its board. He was the executive director of Greater Boston Legal Services, and also the Lawyers' Committee for Civil Rights in Chicago. Through his private practice based in Boston, Bill currently provides legal advice and development expertise to charitable foundations, universities, and new business ventures on four continents.

Peter H. Smyth

Peter H. Smyth says that some of his favorite childhood memories are of when his grandmother, who emigrated from Co. Cork, would read to him with her colorful brogue. The chairman and chief executive officer of Greater Media, Inc., Peter began his career in broadcasting in 1977 as an account executive with WROR-FM in Boston and now oversees a company that includes the operation of 21 AM and FM radio stations in Boston, Charlotte, Detroit, Philadelphia, and New Jersey, as well as a group of weekly newspapers in central New Jersey. He graduated from the College of the Holy Cross in Worcester, Massachusetts, where his parents met when they were students. An active philanthropist, Peter serves on the Board of Directors of New England Baptist Hospital and The Hundred Club of Massachusetts, an organization dedicated to enhancing the welfare and safety of the families of public safety officers and firefighters.

Sister Lena Deevy and Ronnie Millar

When **Sister Lena Deevy**, LSA, and a group of Irish immigrants founded the Irish International Immigrant Center (IIIC) in 1989, they set out to address the needs of those arriving from Ireland. Over the years, IIIC has developed into a multiservice welcome center, serving immigrants from Ireland and 120 other countries with legal, wellness, and education services, learning exchange programs, advocacy, and cross-cultural community building. Sister Lena emigrated from Co. Laois in 1988, and is widely known for her tremendous energy, deep commitment, care, and focus on the mission of helping people. She has been a member of an international order of Catholic women, the Little Sisters of the Assumption, for more than 30 years. She stepped down as executive director in March 2013, and was succeeded by **Ronnie Millar**, who emigrated from Co. Antrim, Northern Ireland in 1993. He previously served as a program manager for Digital Equipment Corporation, the executive director of the South Boston Boys & Girls Club, and as the director of the Corrymeela Peace and Reconciliation Center in Ireland. The IIIC celebrated its 25th anniversary in October 2014 by honoring Sister Lena with the Solas (Gaelic for light) Award. Sister Lena, Ronnie, and the IIIC continue to serve in the Irish spirit and tradition of hospitality, human rights, and care for others, traits for which the Irish are so well known throughout the world.

Scott F. Powers and Debra J. Gould

Debra J. Gould, Scott F. Powers and their seven siblings are proud of their Irish roots and the strong work ethic that was instilled by their family. In fact, they have dedicated their lives to living up to that model in both the business world and in their charitable giving. Their father's parents emigrated from Co. Waterford. Their grandfather worked as a milkman and their father, Andrew K. "Kenny" Powers, worked his way up from a copy boy to picture editor at *The Boston Record* and later at the *Boston Herald*. Deb and Scott's generation were the first to attend college and their parents worked full-time while their children grew up so that the family could afford to pay for their education. Both Deb and Scott are successful in their respective industries. Scott is president and CEO of State Street Global Advisors, where he is also a member of State Street's Management Committee and the Major Risk Committee. Scott attended St. Paul's School and Harvard where he played varsity hockey. Scott has been involved with the United Way for 20 years, has actively supported the American Ireland Fund for 15 years and was chairman of the 2014 Fund gala that raised more than $2.4 million. Deb is an executive director at Cushman & Wakefield, one of a very few prominent women in Boston's commercial real estate industry. She and her husband, John, formed the Gould Family Foundation, which provides support to humanitarian organizations with a priority on underprivileged women and children.

Warren and Steven Tolman

Brothers **Warren** and **Steven Tolman**, who represented Brighton and Watertown and surrounding communities in the Massachusetts House and Senate, are shown here outside the Stockyard restaurant, which is located in the districts they served. Steven and Warren are the sixth and seventh of David and Marie (Tully) Tolman's eight children. The Tolmans started their family just up the road in the Fidelis Way Housing Project just off Commonwealth Avenue in Brighton. Steven (right) is the president of the Massachusetts AFL-CIO, the state's largest labor organization, representing more than 750 local unions. Warren, who attended Amherst College and Boston College Law School, ran unsuccessfully in the Democratic primary for Massachusetts Attorney General in the fall of 2014. The brothers were once introduced at a political event as coming from a large Irish family (their forebears are from Cork and Galway) that is active in politics, just like the Kennedys. To this Warren replied, "That's right. We are a lot like the Kennedys, except for the hair and the money!"

Robert F. White

Robert F. White turned his affable and easygoing manner into a successful career of government affairs, media relations and lobbying in Massachusetts. Bob's great-grandfather John Green came to the United States from Co. Cork, settling first in South Boston and later in Neponset. Bob's early memories include large parties on St. Patrick's Day and the Fourth of July thrown by his musical family, where "all the aunts and uncles sang, some better than others." During the 1970s, Bob served in the Mayor's Office for the City of Boston where he worked for the Youth Activities Commission during the time of court-ordered school busing. Bob spearheaded other special projects for the city, including Bicentennial events such as the Tall Ships, the visit of Queen Elizabeth II, and acting as the liaison with the U.S. Conference of Mayors. After leaving the public sector, Bob was part of the team that worked to create legislation that allowed Kemper Insurance to leave the state while creating Arbella Mutual Insurance Company. This $119-million transaction is credited with salvaging 1,000 Quincy-based jobs.

Philip W. Johnston

Before he was involved in politics, **Philip W. Johnston** began his career in public service. Founder and president of the eponymous health and human services issues consulting firm, Phil began his career as a state child welfare social worker. After campaigning for Senator Robert F. Kennedy in the 1968 presidential election, Phil founded the RFK Children's Action Corps. In 1974, he was elected to the first of four terms in the state House of Representatives. He then was appointed state Secretary of Health and Human Services by Governor Dukakis in 1984, became the executive director of the Robert F. Kennedy Center for Justice and Human Rights in Washington D.C., and subsequently was appointed by President Clinton as the New England Administrator of Health and Human Services. He was also chairman of the Massachusetts Democratic Party from 2000 to 2007. Phil says his ancestors set an example of self-sufficiency. His grandfather Philip W. Johnston emigrated from Sligo with his widowed mother in 1881, but relatives in Worcester who didn't have enough money to feed everyone turned them away, and they had to make their own way.

Edward F. Davis, Kathleen O'Toole and William Bratton

Three former Boston Police Department commissioners—**Edward F. Davis** (left), **Kathleen O'Toole**, and **William Bratton**—were back in town in March 2014 for the inaugural Boston Police Foundation Gala, which provides private financial support to the department. Ed has deep Irish roots in counties Galway and Mayo that date back to the 19th century. His maternal great-grandmother immigrated to Lowell from Co. Mayo in the late 1890s, where she ran a boarding house for Irish immigrants. Ed comes from a law enforcement family and has more than 30 years of law enforcement experience. He is the former superintendent of the Lowell Police Department and served as Boston Police Commissioner from December 2006 to October 2013. During his tenure, he led the department in a successful response to the tragic Boston Marathon bombings. He is the founder and CEO of Edward Davis, LLC, a security and consulting firm based in Boston. The Chief of Police in Seattle, Washington, since June 2014, Kathy served as commissioner from February 2004 to May 2006—the first woman to hold the job—and was also Massachusetts Secretary of Public Safety. During the Irish Peace Process, Kathy served on the Independent Commission on Policing in Northern Ireland, and, more recently, she served as chief inspector of the Garda Síochána, the Irish National Police Service. She traces her roots to Co. Roscommon, and says that she has more relatives there than in America. Bill is the commissioner of the New York City Police Department; it is the second time he has held the position. Bill grew up in an Irish-American household in Dorchester and served as Boston Police Commissioner from 1993 to 1994. He also ran the MBTA police, the former Metropolitan District Commission police, and, from 2002 to 2009, the Los Angeles Police Department.

Pauline Wells

Pauline Wells, a lieutenant for the Cambridge Police Department, began her singing career "by accident," she says, when, with the encouragement of family and friends, she sang at a pub in Cork City, Ireland, in 2000. Shortly after 9/11, Pauline mastered singing the national anthem and has done so at the TD Garden, Fenway Park, veterans and memorial events—making more than 300 public appearances. Known for her melodic renditions of traditional music, Pauline regularly performs with the band Devri. She donates all of her earnings from singing to area charities. Born in Brighton, Pauline grew up in North Cambridge and received degrees from University of Massachusetts and Anna Maria College. She joined the Cambridge Police Department in 1993 and, about 10 years later, was promoted to sergeant detective. In 2010, she attained the rank of lieutenant. In 2006, Pauline was stricken with Acute Hearing Loss that left her unable to hear in her left ear, but her singing continues undiminished.

Michael and John J. McGlynn

The McGlynn family has roots in the Irish counties of Mayo, Sligo, Donegal, and Cork, and, here in the United States, they are known for their public service. **John J. "Jack" McGlynn**'s more than 50 years in public life include being Medford's mayor for 10 years while serving as the city's State Representative. He also was chief secretary to former Governor Ed King. Jack has been recognized for his successful efforts to improve the quality of life for seniors while creating opportunities for the younger generation. During World War II, Jack was a staff sergeant in the U.S. Army as a member of a tactical deception unit known as the Ghost Army, which was credited with saving thousands during the war. Jack's son **Michael** followed in Dad's footsteps after meeting a great Irishman, President John F. Kennedy, on January 9, 1961, at the Massachusetts State House, where Kennedy gave his now famous "The City Upon a Hill" speech. In 1976, the younger McGlynn, a senior at University of Massachusetts Boston, was elected to the state Legislature. Mike was elected mayor in 1987, and he continues as Medford's longest-serving mayor. He also is believed to be the longest-serving mayor in the state. Mike has lead the effort to construct all new elementary and middle schools, as well as expanding Medford's economic base. The McGlynns respect their Irish elders for "always leading by example with warmth and compassion."

Katherine Craven

Raised in West Roxbury, **Katherine Craven** grew up in a staunchly Irish-Catholic household where politics, education, and family shared the highest priority. Her father, Judge John Craven, "always taught me: when the Irish came to Boston, politics was the only way many Irish families could succeed," she says. Katherine's mother, née Patricia McCarthy, has strong family ties to Co. Cork. The family of her grandmother, for whom Katherine was named, came from Co. Derry and raised 11 children. But she didn't stay at home. In 1964, the elder Katherine Craven was the first woman elected citywide to the Boston City Council. Her paternal grandfather, John Craven, with roots in Co. Roscommon, served as state representative from Roxbury. Katherine graduated from Boston Latin and Harvard. She was the founding executive director for the Massachusetts School Building Authority, the first deputy state treasurer for the Commonwealth, and the executive director for the University of Massachusetts Building Authority. In February 2014, Katherine became chief administrative and financial officer at Babson College. She resides in Brookline with her husband, Dr. James Kryzanski, and their four children.

Cindy and Dermot Quinn

When **Dermot Quinn** immigrated to Boston, one of the things he missed most was his Granny Murphy's Irish soda bread. Dermot says that when he saw that many others in the area yearned for the traditional breads and scones that are staples of the Irish diet, he and his wife, **Cindy**, opened Greenhills Bakery in 1991. Dermot attended culinary school in Ireland and got his training at the Great Southern Hotel (now the Hotel Meyrick) in Eire Square, Galway. Cindy, the bakery's cake decorator, graduated from the University of Massachusetts Amherst, Isenberg School of Management. The bakery, which takes its name from Dermot's family homestead in the town of Rhode, Co. Offaly, has become famous for its Guinness beef stew, Irish sausage, rolls, and pastries. Greenhills in Dorchester has become the first stop for many Irish who visit the United States, and it is a regular meeting spot for those who live in the area. Dermot has been lauded for organizing the Irish Heritage Festival in Adams Village, and he and Cindy support neighborhood schools, athletic teams, and charity efforts. It's been said that if you want to find out what's happening among Boston's Irish, Greenhills is the place to go.

Tommy MacDonald

Tommy MacDonald, the charismatic creator and host of WGBH-TV's *Rough Cut: Woodworking with Tommy Mac*, was born the eighth of nine children to hardworking parents in Boston's Dorchester neighborhood. His mom's family emigrated from Tralee in Co. Kerry in the 19th century, while his dad's came over at the turn of the last century from Co. Cork. Over the following 100 years, the families dug deep roots in Boston's traditionally Irish enclaves of Brighton, Roxbury, and South Boston. When a serious work accident ended Tommy's commercial construction career, he went back to school and studied the art of furniture making. Tommy's Irish good looks and his quick-witted sense of humor propelled him from behind the workbench to in front of the camera where a new career as public television's pied piper of woodworking was born. In October 2014, the fifth season of Tommy's show began with an episode featuring a visit to Tommy's workshop by chef Paul Wahlberg.

William J. Geary

William J. Geary's life in public service and politics was set when he was 12 years old and his mother, Mary Geary, took him on election eve 1960 to meet John F. Kennedy. She worked in every city, state, and national political campaign from 1944 to 1988. (Some years later, Bill would take his mother to the same Boston hotel to introduce her to President Clinton.) Bill is third-generation Irish-American. His maternal grandmother, Dora May McDermott, came to Boston from Northern Ireland, and his paternal grandmother, Julia Geary, came to Boston in 1912 from Co. Galway. They both married Irishmen and raised their families in Roxbury and Dorchester. Bill's 15 years in public service included stints in the Dukakis administration and serving as a Commissioner of the Metropolitan District Commission. Bill was then recruited to join Clean Harbors, Inc., where he served as senior vice president and chief legal counsel for more than 20 years and later became president of Clean Harbors Development, a solar power subsidiary.

The Hunt Family

The Hunt Family is solidly Dorchester. Thomas Hunt emigrated from Co. Mayo in 1890 and settled on Houghton Street in Pope's Hill around 1905. His grandson, **James Hunt, Jr.**, standing in front of his sons, was raised nearby by his parents, James and Grace, and when Jim Jr. married his wife, Jean, they too made their home a few doors up the street. Jim is the longtime CEO of the Massachusetts League Community Health Centers. **James III** (left) studied at Saint Ann School (as did all of his brothers) and graduated from Boston Latin School, followed by University of Massachusetts Amherst, and Suffolk Law School. He served as the chief of Environment and Energy in the Menino Administration and now works for Northeast Utilities. **Daniel**,

(center behind his father) is the youngest, and attended Boston Latin Academy, Boston College, the University College of Galway, and Suffolk Law School. Inspired by his studies in Ireland, Daniel ran successfully for state representative in 2014, in the seat previously occupied by Mayor Walsh. **Peter C. Hunt** (far right) graduated from Catholic Memorial High School and Bridgewater State College. Peter worked with Investors Bank and Trust Company and took a financial management assignment in Dublin, Ireland, for two years in 2004. Peter is an insurance executive for New York Life Insurance Company. A fourth brother, Matthew A. Hunt, died in 2002 after a long illness.

Steve Greeley

After nearly 30 years in private law practice, **Steve Greeley** changed careers to become the New England Director of the American Ireland Fund in late summer 2008. Though his timing may not have been fortuitous given the collapse of the U.S. economy, his affinity for Ireland—spawned by his hardworking parents from Somerville, who were proud of their 100-percent Irish ancestral roots—made the challenge all the more attractive. His efforts to strengthen and expand the reach of the American Ireland Fund, whose goals are to raise money for Irish projects and to promote and help people connect with Ireland, have led to record performances in Boston, most visibly by its annual sold-out, black-tie gala dinner. "My great-grandmother, whom I never met, accompanied by my grandmother, who was a young girl at the time, used to 'scrub the floors and toilets on their hands and knees' in the dormitories at the Harvard Law School, which I attended. Today, I like to think they are smiling down on me."

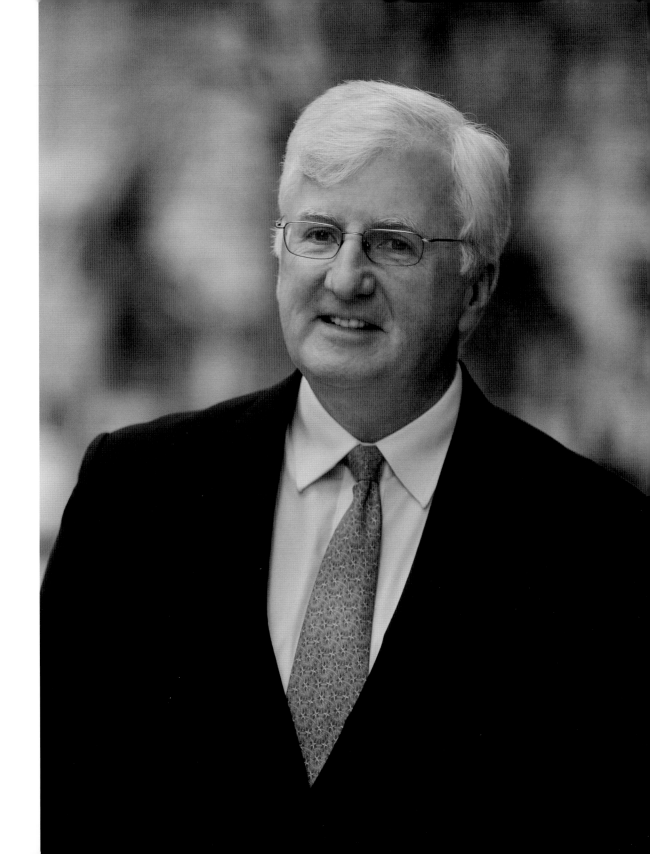

Massachusetts Fallen Heroes Memorial

After serving in the armed forces, these three Boston firefighters—from left, **Ed Kelly**, **Dan Magoon**, and **Greg Kelly**—came together and are leading the charge to honor those who have lost their lives in Iraq and Afghanistan in service to their country. In October 2014, there was a ceremony to break ground on the $6.5-million Massachusetts Fallen Heroes Memorial Park in South Boston's Seaport Square, which is being built in partnership with John B. Hynes III, Boston Global Investors, the Commonwealth of Massachusetts, and Morgan Stanley. It will be the first of its kind in the nation. The three men behind The Massachusetts Iraq and Afghanistan Fallen Heroes Memorial Fund were photographed at the Engine 21 firehouse. A firefighter assigned to Ladder 17, Ed is president of The Professional Firefighters of Massachusetts, a director of Mass Fallen Heroes and a U.S. Air Force veteran. Executive Director of Mass Fallen Heroes, Dan is a firefighter with Engine 21 and a U.S. Army combat veteran. Greg, who is Ed's brother, is president of Mass Fallen Heroes, a firefighter assigned to Tower Ladder 10, and a U.S. Army combat veteran. "We are just regular Irish-Catholic Americans who served our country," Dan says. "We wanted to do this for the families of the fallen, following in the footsteps of the generations of veterans before us." The Kelly family is from Dorchester and traces its history back to the Ireland counties of Limerick and Donegal. Dan's family comes from Co. Galway, other parts of Ireland, and Scotland.

Mary Joyce Morris

Born in Galway City, Ireland, **Mary Joyce Morris** came to Boston as a toddler. Her parents, Michael and Theresa Helebert Joyce, raised six children in St. Margaret's Parish, Dorchester, with the three Rs: respect, responsibility, and religion. Mary has been involved with numerous charitable organizations, and she says none has been more satisfying than leading the efforts to remember the legacy of her late father, who served under four Massachusetts House Speakers. The Michael Joyce Memorial Playground (shown behind Mary) was dedicated in 2010, and is located in South Boston at Marine Park, which was designed by Frederick Law Olmsted. In 2014, in partnership with the Department of Conservation and Recreation, the playground was renovated and expanded with equipment accessible for children with disabilities and a new toddler lot. "My father spent his life helping others," says Mary. "He never asked a person's race, color, or creed. He would only say, 'How can I help?' and this park keeps that spirit alive."

Peg and Fred Rooney

Fred and **Peg "Hon" Rooney** are shown with Bill Brett's second book, *Boston, An Extended Family*, open to the pages on which the photograph of their 11 sons appears. The Rooney sons—Jim, Joe, Larry, Paul, Michael, Chris, Tommy, Buddy, Jay, Jackie and Mark—are shown seated at the Dorchester Heights National Historic Site in South Boston. The park is around the corner from the Gate Street home where Fred and Hon live and raised their sons. It is also the house where Hon was raised by her parents, Bridget "Delia" (Waldron), who came to Boston at age 15 from Co. Mayo, and Michael Corliss, who left Tuam, Co. Galway, at age 17. Fred's grandparents Margaret Laverey and Stephen Curran emigrated from Co. Galway. Fred worked primarily in the trucking industry but often worked two and three jobs while his wife worked nights doing data processing—all to support the family. The couple's efforts paid off: four of their sons have Ivy League degrees and all 11 have achieved notable success in their chosen fields, which include business, real estate, government, sports, and education.

Thomas G. Kelley, Thomas J. Hudner, Jr., and Tom Lyons

On the morning that this photograph was taken, **Thomas G. Kelley** (left) and **Thomas J. Hudner, Jr.**, both recipients of the Medal of Honor, were interested in making contact with New Hampshire's Ryan M. Pitts, a former U.S. staff sergeant who was about to receive the Medal of Honor for his combat actions in Afghanistan. "It is a pretty exclusive group," says **Tom Lyons** (right). A Dorchester native who grew up in West Roxbury, Tom Kelley received the Medal of Honor for his actions in Vietnam in 1969 when he led eight boats to extract a U.S. Army infantry company. His great-grandfather, for whom he's named, left Ireland for America and enlisted a short time later in the Union Army. He retired as a captain in 1990 and later served as commissioner of the state Department of Veterans' Services. Tom Hudner's family left Ireland and made their way to Fall River, where they ran Hudner's Markets. A graduate of the U.S. Naval Academy, Tom was an aviator in the Korean War who was awarded the Medal of Honor for trying to save the life of his wingman, Ensign Jesse L. Brown. He retired as a captain in 1973 and served as commissioner of the state Department of Veterans' Services prior to Tom Kelley. The Arleigh Burke-class guided missile destroyer *USS Thomas Hudner* is currently being built in Bath, Maine, and will be commissioned in his honor. A South Boston native and U.S. Marine Corps veteran of the Vietnam War, Tom Lyons is founder and chairman of the nonprofit Boston Semper Fidelis Society and works with the Medal of Honor recipients. His family hails from Co. Cork.

Barbara Whelan, Marie Keough, and Barbara Scanlon

In the late 1960s, three young teachers (from left), **Barbara Whelan**, **Marie Keough**, and **Barbara Scanlon**, who were also members of the Sisters of St. Joseph in Boston, began reaching out to troubled youth on Boston Common and in Cambridge. That work led these three Irish-Americans to open Bridge Over Troubled Waters in 1970. At first, the Sisters provided sandwiches, cold drinks, and nonjudgmental conversations that turned into supportive counseling, referrals for health care, psychiatric services, a way back home, and planning for alternatives when returning home was not an option. Their first summer, more than 1,000 young people living on the streets of Boston were helped by the fledgling organization.

Each woman took on a role to run the Boston-based nonprofit: Sister Barbara Whelan, founding executive director; Sister Marie Keough, financial director; and Sister Barbara Scanlon, head outreach worker and program director. With physicians from Massachusetts General Hospital, they organized a volunteer-run Mobile Medical Van—the first of its kind in the nation—and they were on the forefront of a national movement, which led to the passage of the Runaway and Homeless Youth Act in 1974. Today, Bridge serves more than 3,000 at-risk young people each year in a multiservice system that ranges from street outreach and emergency services to long-term counseling, education, and transitional housing.

Robert K. Sheridan

Robert K. Sheridan, philanthropist and former president and CEO of SBLI of Massachusetts, traces his Irish roots to his grandfather John J. Sheridan, who was born in Co. Offaly and immigrated to Boston in 1883. Bob retired in 2012 after 20 years as SBLI's chief executive, having overseen the company's growth from one state into a national company. Bob and his wife, Jean O'Hara Sheridan, whose family hailed from Co. Sligo, are supporters of a number of charities. He is pictured inside the Massachusetts Affordable Housing Alliance's Robert and Jean Sheridan Homeownership Building in Dorchester. The building was named in recognition of his role in chairing the capital campaign that raised $3.5 million for its construction. His service to the University of Massachusetts as a trustee and chairman of the Building Authority is acknowledged each year with the awarding of the Robert and Jean O'Hara Sheridan Scholarship to UMass Boston undergraduates who are residents of Boston, Jamaica Plain, and Everett.

Kevin O'Connor

Like so many others before him, *This Old House* host **Kevin O'Connor** came to the Boston area for college and chose to stay after graduation. A New Jersey native, he graduated from the College of the Holy Cross and later received a master's of business administration from Boston University. Kevin worked for Bank of America as a senior vice president in the Commercial Real Estate Group and previously in the Sports Finance Group at Fleet Bank. When Kevin, a lifelong fan of *This Old House*, and his wife, Kathleen, were renovating their 1892 Queen Anne Victorian, they sent an e-mail to the PBS show's experts seeking advice. The experts responded, and that "house call" served as Kevin's screen test. He has hosted the show for 12 years. Kevin's paternal great-grandparents emigrated from Sligo and Mayo. His mother's family came from Ireland through Ellis Island, and their hometowns were not recorded.

AJ Gerriston

Marketing expert **AJ Gerriston**'s family story in Boston reads like an Edwin O'Connor novel. With family roots tracing back to Cos. Cavan and Cork, AJ counts among his ancestors a Boston fire chief, a great-grandmother who was a first cousin to Mayor James Michael Curley, and a great-great-grandfather who died after a fall during the construction of Metropolitan Theater (now the Citi Wang Theater). His family also remembers an act of kindness in the 1930s, by then-acting Police Commissioner Joseph F. Timilty, that kept them from losing everything. AJ is on the board of the Charitable Irish Society, and chairman of the board for the Boston Irish Business Association. AJ was captain of the University of Massachusetts Amherst's men's rugby team and later played professionally in Limerick, Ireland. In 2004, he cofounded 451 Marketing, which has grown to become of the largest communications agencies in New England, with 70 employees and offices in New York and Los Angeles.

Steve Connelly

You can often spy **Steve Connelly** wearing a scally cap like the one in this photograph—his "favorite," purchased on recent trip to Dublin. His father's family hails from Co. Cork, and Steve counts Ireland among his favorite places to visit. He proudly notes that his grandfather was an accomplished Irish fiddler. Steve is shown near a brick archway outside the South End headquarters of Connelly Partners, one of New England's largest integrated marketing firms. As founder and president of the company that bears his name, Steve oversaw the tremendous growth of his firm with eight strategic mergers and acquisitions over the last 15 years. He did so while keeping the core culture of his business intact. Steve has a full-service bar in the middle of his office space, perhaps expected for an Irishman. But Steve doesn't drink and never has, perhaps unexpected. The bar, he says, gives the more than 100 people who work at Connelly Partners a place to gather, much like the kitchen table in most Irish homes.

Carolyn A. and Peter S. Lynch

In the 25 years since **Carolyn A. Lynch** and **Peter S. Lynch** launched The Lynch Foundation, with a belief that they can affect the change they want to see in their community, they have given out more than $80 million in grants to nonprofits. The couple support a number of Boston charities in the areas of education, health care, museums, and religious institutions, including the Catholic Schools Foundation, College Bound Dorchester, and the Ron Burton Training Village. In October 2014, the family foundation gave the St. Joseph Preparatory School in Boston a $750,000 grant to build a new academic center. "Looking back, I was damned lucky. I won the lottery," Peter told *The Boston Globe*. "We're just trying to give the same opportunities to other children.

…Some people think public schools are hopeless. We don't think that is true. We think they can get a lot better." Peter, who has been recognized by several publications as one of the country's leading Irish-Americans in the field of finance, became a household name from his 13 years of generating awe-inspiring returns at the helm of Fidelity's Magellan Fund. He applies that same business acumen to overseeing the family foundation's investment committee. Carolyn, who serves as the foundation's president and CEO, offers this bit of advice on the foundation's website: "Discover where your passion lies. Act on it. And you will accomplish great things."

Tom "Red" Martin

With all the accomplishments that **Tom "Red" Martin** has achieved, you would think he has lived two lifetimes. From a young age, Tom excelled as a hockey player, first at Cambridge High and Latin, where he also was a standout baseball and football player, and then at Boston College, where he was captain of the hockey team that won two Beanpot championships. He was assistant captain of the 1964 U.S. Olympic hockey team and was drafted by the Boston Bruins, a contract that he turned down so that he could make a better living as an accountant. Tom later bought a five-person division of the electronics firm where he worked and turned it into Cramer Electronics, which has more than 200 employees, including six of Tom's seven children with wife, June. Tom's grandfather Thomas Considine left Co. Clare for America and arrived in Boston Harbor onboard the *Gallia* in 1897. Those humble beginnings drive Tom to support a slate of charitable efforts, he says, which include the Massachusetts Hospital School and Ouimet Foundation.

Therese Murray

Growing up in St. Mark's Parish in Dorchester as one of six children, Massachusetts Senate President **Therese Murray** learned the traditional Irish values of hard work, community and helping others from her mother and father. A self-described bologna-and-cheese Democrat, she cut her political teeth working for Senator Ted Kennedy's first run for the U.S. Senate. Throughout her career, Terry has embraced the OFD (Originally from Dorchester) title and has never forgotten the values instilled in her by her parents. In 1992, she successfully beat a 20-year incumbent to become a state senator. From there, she rose through the ranks in the State House to chair of Senate Ways and Means and, in 2007, to the president of the Massachusetts Senate. Terry's ties to Ireland go beyond her economic development efforts. Her family tree stretches across the island with family names including Harrold and Conners from Dublin; Edwards from Cork; Kelley from Limerick; Hickey from Galway; and Harrold from Belfast, Northern Ireland.

Cornelia Cassidy Koutoujian

Cornelia Cassidy Koutoujian remembers well that when her children were growing up in Waltham, they attended the Armenian language school Saturdays and took Irish step dance lessons every Wednesday. "My husband, Peter, and I embraced each other's ethnicity without diminishing either," Connie says of her 54-year marriage. All four of Connie's grandparents came to Boston from Ireland at the turn of the last century: The O'Connors, Spillanes, and Hurleys from West Cork, and the Cassidys from Galway. She was named for her paternal grandfather, and through him she obtained her Irish citizenship. Growing up in Newton near her grandparents meant that Connie was surrounded by Irish music—on the old record player and the sheet music on the piano in the living room. Connie is involved with numerous civic and cultural groups, including the Irish International Immigrant Center and the Eire Society of Boston. In 2002, she received the Silver Key Award from the Charitable Irish Society.

Seamus Mulligan

Listening to **Seamus Mulligan**'s Sunday afternoon radio show *Feast of Irish Music* on WROL-AM is a bit like sitting at a kitchen table with friends and having a cup of tea. For four hours every week, Seamus weaves music, stories, news, history and cultural lore together for a show that has a devoted following. Born in Monaghan, Seamus lived in Manorhamilton, Co. Leitrim, and Tullamore, Co. Offaly, and completed first- and second-level education in Ireland before moving to the United States in 1959. He and his wife, Mary Ellen (Welch), live in Randolph and have four grown children. The family has participated in countless Irish cultural events over the years. Seamus also has been involved in numerous Irish organizations holding leadership positions, including past president and director of the Irish Cultural Centre Inc. and chairman of the Centre's annual festivals.

Doris Kearns Goodwin

Doris Kearns Goodwin, Pulitzer Prize-winning presidential biographer and historian, cites her own family's story for inspiring her view on how history is recorded. "My father was the son of Irish immigrants. His accounts of his heritage and his family's struggle to establish a place for themselves in a strange, harsh and promising land, had illuminated my childhood musings and fueled my young ambition," she told the authors of the 2006 book *Making the Irish American*. *The New York Times* best-selling author's most recent book, *The Bully Pulpit: Theodore Roosevelt, William Howard Taft, and the Golden Age of Journalism*, was released in late 2013. Her critically-acclaimed *Team of Rivals: The Political Genius of Abraham Lincoln*, was the basis for Steven Spielberg's Academy Award-winning film, *Lincoln*. Doris received her doctorate from Harvard and worked for President Johnson in his last year in office. Doris is married to Richard N. Goodwin, a presidential adviser, writer, speechwriter and playwright. She is the first woman to have entered the Boston Red Sox locker room, and "is a devoted fan of the World Series-winning team."

John Stenson

John Stenson, owner of the Eire Pub, greeted the assembling crowd gathering for the September 16, 2014, celebration that marked the 50th anniversary of the Adams Village destination that has played host to U.S. Presidents Ronald Reagan and Bill Clinton and numerous politicians and celebrities. The Eire Pub was opened by John's father, Thomas C. Stenson, who died in 2000, and remains a regular stop for neighbors and those who live in the suburbs, who crowd around the horseshoe-shaped bar waiting for a draught and a "dog." John's family has roots in counties Sligo, Clare, and Mayo, and his parents met at a club that Tom was operating in Everett. When Tom opened the Eire Pub, he put up the famous signs, "Men's Bar" and "Gentlemen's Prestige Bar." "Eire Pub and Locke-Ober were the last two places that were licensed to operate that way," John says. "We're open to everyone now, so the sign confuses people. The historic preservation folks won't let me change it, so it stays."

Edmund F. Murphy

Edmund F. Murphy III, head of Putnam Investments' retirement business, takes great pride in his family's immigrant story and, as chairman of the 2013 Boston Irish Honors, has celebrated the community's success. In fact, John's late uncle Jack Driscoll, the famed attorney who helped countless Boston residents, was among the leading Irish citizens honored that year. Ed's story in America begins with his maternal grandmother, Mary Sullivan, from Castletownbere, a small town on the Beara Peninsula, Co. Cork, and his grandfather John P. Driscoll of the tiny village of Eyeries, about seven kilometers away. The couple actually met when they both were at a dance in Hibernian Hall in Roxbury. Prior to joining Putnam, Ed spent 17 years with Fidelity Investments and held numerous executive and senior management level positions. Born in Boston, Ed graduated from Boston College. He is an active volunteer with Boston Healthcare for the Homeless Program, Cristo Rey Boston High School in Dorchester, the American Ireland Fund, and many other charitable organizations.

Dick Flavin

Author and playwright **Dick Flavin** is the poet laureate and senior ambassador of the Boston Red Sox and voice of Fenway Park. Dick is a nationally known speaker and is in the Massachusetts Broadcasters Hall of Fame. Dick's commentaries during his years at WBZ-TV in Boston won seven New England Regional Emmy Awards. He is among the few people who can claim having been a friend of both Ted Williams and Ted Kennedy. "If you hang around politics and baseball long enough, that's what happens," he says. Dick has written and performed scores of verses and ballads about the Red Sox, their iconic ballpark, and their storied players. His work is being turned into a book, due out in 2015. Dick is full-blooded Irish with roots in Cork and Kerry, and if you look up his name in Wikipedia, it says that he was the goalkeeper for the Co. Cork team in the Irish Football League in the early 20th century. "I guess that must have been me," Dick jokes. "I don't exactly remember it, but there are lots of things I don't remember."

The Mulligan Family

As much as the Mulligan family is proud of the story of their ancestors leaving Co. Cork beginning in 1896 to make a new, better life in America, this West Roxbury family was raised to not be wistful about the past. "My grandfather, Tom, was born in Ireland, but like many immigrants, he had a greater love for America than the people born here," **Robert A. Mulligan** (left) told the *Boston Irish Reporter*. "So, did he have that nostalgic, rosy view of lost opportunities in Ireland? No." That hasn't stopped the family members from achieving success. Bob is a retired chief justice of the Trial Courts of Massachusetts, who served on the bench for 33 years, first in Boston Municipal Court and as chief justice of Superior Court before overseeing administration and management of all the courts in the state.

He retired in July 2013. **Joe Mulligan III**, flanked by his two uncles, is deputy director of Boston's Capital Construction Department. He represents his late father in more than just name. It was said that Joseph I. Mulligan, Jr., who died on April 2, 2008, at age 68, was the most Irish member of the family, having traveled to Ireland more than 30 times. Joe Jr. was Boston's licensing commissioner and the city's corporation counsel. **Gerry Mulligan** (right) attended Boston Latin, the College of the Holy Cross, Georgetown University Law Center, and Harvard Business School. Gerry's banking career included serving as Massachusetts Commissioner of Banks and as president of First Mutual of Boston, Andover Bancorp, and LSB Corporation.

Thomas Clifford

If you've been to an Irish event in the Boston area in the last few decades, chances are you've seen **Thomas Clifford** and his camera filming for his television show *Ireland on the Move*. "It has been my passion to bring Irish culture to TV," Tom says. Tom was born in Killorglin, Co. Kerry, one of six children to John and Mary (McCarthy). When Tom was age nine, his family moved to his mother's hometown of Ennistymon, Co. Clare. His father died when Tom was 13, and a year later Tom rode his bike nearly 26 kilometers to Ennis and pretended to be his older brother Michael to get a job at a quarry busting up rocks with a hammer. He came to the United States in 1957 and moved to Boston in 1963. He met Agnes McGovern from Co. Cavan a short time later; they married and had three children and three grandchildren. Active with the Gaelic Athletic Association in Boston, Tom also has been involved with Boston area political campaigns and lobbied for civil rights of the Irish people in the North.

Kerry Murphy Healey

Babson College President **Kerry Murphy Healey**'s grandfather Edward Morris Murphy emigrated from Co. Cork at the turn of the 20th century, eventually settling in Minneapolis, Minnesota. In 1982, Kerry graduated from Harvard with an A.B. in government. She was then awarded a Rotary International Scholarship and chose to study at Trinity College, Dublin, where she earned a doctorate in political science and law in 1991. She returned to Massachusetts to work at Abt Associates in Cambridge as a criminal justice consultant to the U.S. Department of Justice. Seeking an opportunity to turn her research into policy, she set her sights on the State House, but, contrary to the traditions of Irish politicians in Massachusetts, she ran as a Republican. After two runs for state representative and a stint as chairman of the Massachusetts Republican Party, she joined Mitt Romney's ticket as the lieutenant governor candidate in their victorious 2002 campaign. She served as the 70th lieutenant governor of Massachusetts before running unsuccessfully for governor in 2006.

Joyce A. Murphy

The importance of caring and compassion was learned early on by **Joyce A. Murphy** and five of her siblings when their brother Brian was diagnosed as a child with the rare genetic disorder Hunter syndrome. Joyce says that although Brian died young, she saw how her family rallied to keep the boy in their home and cared for by the immediate family until his death. Now executive vice chancellor at University of Massachusetts Medical School, Joyce says those lessons stay with her working in health care. Previously, she was president of Carney Hospital for nine years, senior vice president of government relations for the Caritas Christi Health Care System, and vice president of St. Margaret's Hospital for Women in Dorchester. Joyce's maternal grandparents met in Boston, but both were from Co. Galway; Delia Kelly came from Ballinasloe and Matthias Kelly from Oughterard. Her paternal grandparents, Dennis Patrick Murphy (Co. Cork) and Catherine (Kelly) Murphy (Co. Kerry), also immigrated at a young age.

Dorchester Parish Priests

Reverend **Richard "Doc" Conway** (left), Right Reverend **Jack Ahern** (center), and Reverend **Dan Finn**—all Roman Catholic priests in Dorchester—say it is altogether fitting that their photograph was taken on Mount Ida Road at Bowdoin Street next to the St. Peter convent. The three men have connections to and served in many of the Dorchester parishes: St. Mark's, St. Ambrose, Blessed Mother Teresa (St. Margaret's), Holy Family and one that the priests say has a special place in their hearts—St. Peter's. Known as the "church of immigrants," St. Peter's Church was constructed by the newly arrived Irish laborers. The first pastor, Monsignor Ronan, was responsible for building St. Margaret Hospital within the parish. Father Doc grew up in Roslindale. His father, James, was an obstetrician, and his mother, Mary Campbell, was a homemaker who grew up in St. Peter's Parish. Father Doc's grandfather came from Co. Galway. Father Jack was raised in Arlington, one of seven children. His father worked in a produce market and his mother was a teacher. "We grew up proud of our roots in Co. Cork and filled with the sense that all good things were possible for us," Father Jack says. Father Dan, his parents and six siblings were all born in Co. Cork and immigrated to Lowell, Massachusetts. He arrived in America at the age of 18. For many years, Father Dan has been the go-to priest for the Irish who have newly arrived in the United States.

Kevin Gill

Kevin Gill, president and sole owner of McCusker-Gill, Inc. a Hingham-based heating and air-conditioning contractor, attributes his company's considerable success to his employees. President of the Boston branch of the Sheet Metal and Air Conditioning Contractors' National Association, Kevin is very involved in the Sheet Metal Workers Local 17 and was recognized in 2004 as the contractor of the year by an industry group. But Kevin says it is family and strong Irish-Catholic values that guide him and his wife, Rita, his high school sweetheart, as they raise their six children, Kevin Jr., Marianne, Stephanie, Patrick, Christine and Elizabeth. Kevin's father, Patrick Gill, was first generation Irish-American, born to parents who emigrated from Co. Cork and raised their family in Roxbury. Kevin's mother, Margaret (Boyle), was born in Ballybunion and came to the United States at age 26, seeking a way out of poverty. She worked as a nanny and sent money back to her family in Ireland and took great pride in becoming a U.S. citizen.

The Monahan Family

Marion (Whalen) Monahan proves the saying that you should never underestimate the toughness of a hockey mom. Marion is shown here in her South Boston living room with her sons, who are (from left): **Kevin Patrick**, **Terence Francis**, **Robert Daniel**, **Daniel Thomas**, and **Sean Joseph**. Marion, a cofounder of South Boston Youth Hockey, professes her love of hockey on the walls of her house—photographs of Pope Francis and his three predecessors and Boston Cardinals Richard Cushing and Seán O'Malley share space with Bobby Orr, John McKenzie, and Terry O'Reilly. (The picture of O'Reilly, Marion's favorite, is hung one inch higher than all the others.) Marion's late husband, Bob, a sports writer at *The Boston Globe* for almost 50 years, was the first athletic director of the Gate of Heaven CYO. Bob's late brother, D. Leo Monahan, a sportswriter at the *Herald*, *Globe*, and other publications, is in the Hockey Hall of Fame. Her boys inherited her determination and sense of community pride by being engaged in issues that can make a difference. All of them, and now their children, have been active members of their community as coaches, referees, nonprofit workers, community activists, and organizers. The family's roots in South Boston go back a few generations. Bob Monahan was born on Seventh Street where he and Marion raised their five sons. His family came to the United States from Carlow, Limerick, and Portarlington, Co. Laois. Marion's family came to Gate of Heaven parish through Ellis Island from Co. Cork and Killeshandra, Co. Cavan.

The Flaherty Family

Francis X. "Frank" Flaherty, shown here with his three sons, was born in the three-family house (in background) at 67 Arlington Street in Brighton to Peter and Nora (Kelly) Flaherty, who emigrated from Oughterard, Co. Galway. Nora arrived in Boston first, in 1921 at age 23, and Peter followed her a year later. She worked as a cook for a family on Beacon Hill, and he was a bricklayer. They made their home for 30 years in that house in St. Columbkille's Parish. His parents' formidable work ethic stayed with Frank, who is an attorney and former Middlesex County Commissioner. He met his wife, Maureen, at the nearby St. Elizabeth's Hospital, where she worked as a nurse for 35 years. The couple, who have been married for 52 years, have three sons and 10 grandchildren. The sons are, from left, **Peter G. Flaherty, II**, cofounder of political consulting firm The Shawmut Group, adviser to Governor Mitt Romney and U.S. Senator Scott Brown, and former Suffolk County prosecutor. **Francis X. "Chip" Flaherty, Jr.**, is executive vice president of Walden Media, and **Micheal Flaherty** is cofounder and president of Walden Media, a production company dedicated to family-friendly entertainment. The company's movies include: *Charlotte's Web*, *The Chronicles of Narnia* series, *Journey to the Center of the Earth*, *Holes*, and *The Giver*.

David J. McGillivray

As race director of the Boston Athletic Association's Boston Marathon for 27 years, **David J. McGillivray** knows every inch of the Hopkinton-to-Boston course, which he has run 42 consecutive times, finishing the last 27 at night after his race duties were completed. For the 2014 running, the first since the bombings the year before that claimed three lives and wounded hundreds near the finish line, Dave and his team worked with the city and state to ensure that the thousands of runners and tens of thousands of spectators felt safe and enjoyed the day. Dave is probably best known nationally for his 3,452-mile trek across the United States for the Jimmy Fund that finished in Fenway Park before a Red Sox game in 1978. This father of five has helped raise millions of dollars for numerous local charitable causes. Dave's father, Francis, has Scottish ancestry and his mother, Jacqueline (Eaton), is of Irish descent. His athletic family has always been "short in stature, prompting friends to kid that we're leprechauns."

Robert E. and Maureen Kerwin Kelly

Robert E. Kelly, Jr. was just 33 and had recently founded an office furnishings company in the Seaport District when he was diagnosed with Stage 3 Hodgkin's lymphoma—a diagnosis made all the more difficult because he and his wife, **Maureen Kerwin Kelly**, had lost their fathers at young ages to cancer. More than 20 years later, Bob is in remission and credits his recovery to Dr. Roger Lange, an oncologist at the Beth Israel Deaconess Medical Center who, in a cruel twist, died in early 2012 from multiple myeloma, a disease he spent his career trying to cure. Bob and Maureen turned a family golf vacation to Ireland in 1994 into a 20-year crusade, raising some $1 million via their Drive Fore A Cure. Proceeds first aided Dr. Lange's research and now fund medical training to ensure that the devoted doctor's work continues. Bob is the CEO of Privet Walls and Maureen works in residential real estate after a successful career in the banking industry. The couple, who have three grown children, credit "the Irish-Catholic spirit of their parents and grandparents" (Cork, Galway, Laois and Mayo) with guiding them throughout their lives.

Leslie King-Grenier

In the nearly 40 years since **Leslie King-Grenier** embarked on her career in charitable fundraising and event planning, one project stands out. "The most poignant memory is of working on and arranging events for President Clinton's first visit to Northern Ireland," Leslie says. Her career started in the Boston Office of Cultural Affairs in the White Administration where she was assigned to organize city events for the Bicentennial, including Queen Elizabeth II's first visit to Boston. Later, she was hired by the American Ireland Fund's former Executive Director Kingsley Aikins to be the nonprofit's national fundraising events director. Leslie retired from this position in 2005 and subsequently joined the American Ireland Fund Board. Her family story in America begins when Leslie's grandmother Lillian Willis, who was born in Ireland, came through Ellis Island in the 19th century to work as a nanny for a wealthy widower in Brooklyn. She and the widower fell in love, married and had Leslie's mother and two other daughters.

David O'Shaughnessy

As president and managing director of the Seaport Hotel & World Trade Center in Boston, **David O'Shaughnessy** oversees a 200,000-square-foot facility, Four Diamond hotel, with 2,300 parking spaces that sometimes has the population of a small city. David was born in the village of Adare, Co. Limerick, where his father, Tom, was a local veterinary surgeon for 50 years until his death. David and his wife, Kay, also from Adare, have three grown children. Educated by Irish Christian Brothers and by Diocesan priests at St. Munchin's College, Limerick, David graduated from College of Hotel Management at Shannon, Co. Clare. David began his career at Walkers Cay Resort, located in the Bahamas, which was owned by Robert Abplanalp, a close friend of President Nixon. David says he was fortunate to meet and interact with the president, who was a frequent visitor to the resort.

John E. Drew

As founder and president of the Boston–based real estate management and development company that bears his name, and chairman of Trade Center Management Associates, **John E. Drew** was a pioneer in the development of the South Boston's Seaport District. John founded The Drew Company in 1982, and the company's projects include development of the 2.5-million-square-foot Seaport Hotel and World Trade Center Boston complex and the 3-million-square-foot Ronald Reagan Building in Washington, D.C. A second–generation Irish American and Boston native, John was recognized by Irish America on its "Business 100" list in 2013. He is chairman of the board of the Boston Municipal Research Bureau and chairman of the Cathedral High School trustees. A graduate of Stonehill College and Boston University, John is a member of the American Ireland Fund and serves on the boards of the Greater Boston Chamber of Commerce and Stonehill College.

Mary Beth McMahon

As president and CEO of Special Olympics Massachusetts, **Mary Beth McMahon** has dedicated her professional life to Special Olympics. She sees a direct link to her work in another Irish American, Special Olympics founder Eunice Kennedy Shriver. (Mary Beth is seen in front of a mural at the Special Olympics state headquarters in Marlborough, the site of Mrs. Shriver's famous "You Have Earned It" speech, which she delivered at the World Games in 1987.) A Boston native, this mother of two has been involved with Special Olympics since 1983, first as a volunteer then, after a short stint in the financial industry, full-time in Maryland. She has held a variety of posts, including tenures in Northern California and Nevada, before returning to Massachusetts in 2011. Her professional work has taken Mary Beth closer to her heritage. Both sets of her grandparents were born and raised in Ireland, and Mary Beth's grandmother Mary Hunt, a unifying figure in this large family, lived on Forest Hills Street in Jamaica Plain until her death in 2013 at age 101. It was Mary, a native of the village of Kilflynn in Co. Kerry, who led a group of 40 family members on a return trip to Ireland in 2003 for the Special Olympics World Summer Games.

Jon Cronin

Photographed in his Northern Avenue office in South Boston's Seaport District, **Jon Cronin** is just down the street from Whiskey Priest, a Cronin Group pub whose Gaelic signs announce the food and good times to be found inside. Joe was born in Ballinhassing, Co. Cork, earned his bachelor's degree in structural engineering in 1991 from the University of Massachusetts Lowell and worked at Metcalf & Eddy before entering in the hospitality industry, according to *SouthBostonOnline*. Joe and his partners opened Boston Beer Garden in 1995 and have since grown the business to multiple locations, with more than 1,000 employees working for the Cronin Group. Jon's company has also done $100 million of residential, commercial and retail development, primarily in South Boston. Jon and his wife, Nicole, support a number of charities; he is a member of the board of the South Boston Neighborhood House and the South Boston Collaborative Center.

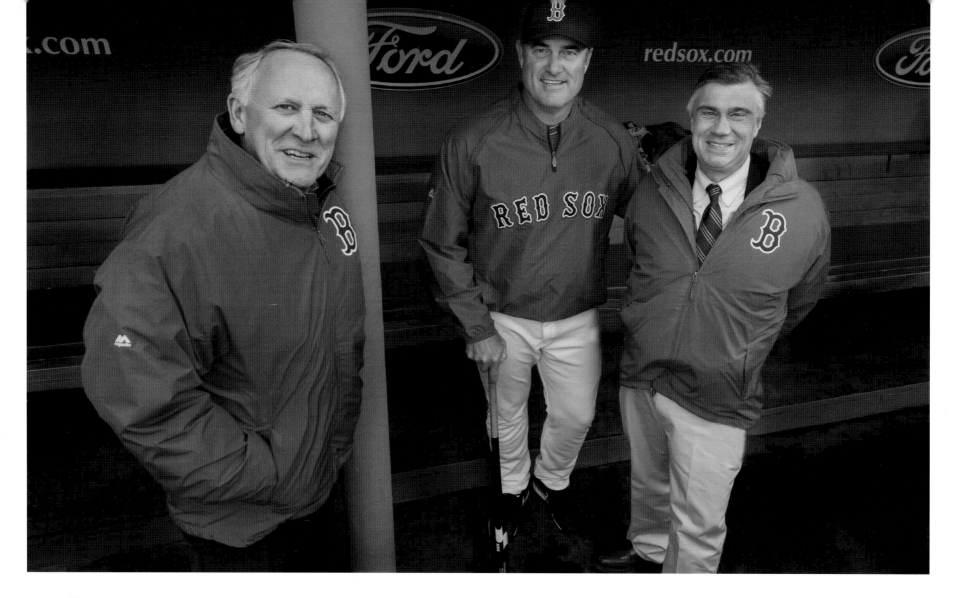

Jack McCormick, John Farrell and Dr. Larry Ronan

When **John Farrell** (center) was named manager of the Red Sox in October 2012, he became the 20th manager of Irish heritage to run the team. The American Ireland Fund honored him a short time after the announcement at the 2012 Gala. The former pitcher returned to Boston from Toronto, where he managed the Blue Jays from 2011 to 2012 and was previously the Red Sox pitching coach from 2007 to 2010. A former Boston police officer, **Jack McCormick** has been the team's traveling secretary since 1996. A lifelong Bostonian, with roots in Jamaica Plain and Roslindale, Jack served in the U.S. Army. His forebears emigrated from Co. Galway in the 1840s. Dr. **Larry Ronan** is the team's medical director and head team internist. A graduate of Harvard University and Harvard Medical School, Larry is an internist at

Massachusetts General Hospital, where he is director of the Dr. Thomas S. Durant Fellowship for Refugee Medicine, which sends medical personnel to troubled spots around the world. Larry's maternal grandmother, Marjorie Jordan, was born in Cork in 1885 and immigrated sometime in the early 20th century to New York City. His paternal grandfather was from Co. Mayo and left Ireland for Baltimore before settling in Iowa in the mid-19th century. Fenway Park itself even has ties to Ireland. The construction of Fenway Park, more than 100 years ago, was led by Charles E. Logue, who was born in Co. Derry, and founded the Logue Building Company, which is still in business today as Logue Engineering. Fenway Park has played host to Gaelic Athletic Association football and hurling matches.

Commander Sean D. Kearns and Commander Robert L. Gillen

Standing on the deck of the *USS Constitution* are U.S. Navy Commander **Sean D. Kearns** (left) and Commander **Robert L. Gillen** (retired), two of the 73 men who have been at the helm of the oldest commissioned naval vessel, which is oft-called "Old Ironsides" after withstanding withering cannon fire in several wars. The three-masted frigate was built in Boston and launched on October 21, 1797. (On October 17, 2014, the storied ship took a sail around Boston Harbor and back to the Charlestown Navy Yard before undergoing a three-year restoration.) Sean is the 73rd and current commanding officer of the *USS Constitution*, where he was commissioned as an ensign in 1994 after his graduation from Boston University. During his Naval career, Sean served nearly 10 years of sea duty on six ships, including the *Constitution*. Born in Bangor, Maine, Sean's family traces its roots to his great-great grandparents: Michael Kearns, born in Dublin, and Ellen McDonnell, from Co. Cork, who were a couple but traveled separately to America in the 1850s. Sean's parents, David and Carolyn, made Maine their home after Sean's father left the U.S. Air Force. All of Bob Gillen's grandparents were from Ireland; his mother's family hailed from Co. Cork, and his father's from Co. Donegal. They settled in Charlestown, where Bob was born and raised. He enlisted in the U.S. Navy in 1951, and his service included duty with Commander Cruiser Destroyer Forces Atlantic, the Third Marines in Danang, Vietnam. In 1978, he returned to Charlestown to become the 59th commanding officer of *USS Constitution*—the first "townie" to be so honored.

Desmond MacIntyre

Under the leadership of Chairman and CEO **Desmond MacIntyre**, the assets of Standish Mellon Asset Management Co. have grown from approximately $40 billion in 2010 to $166 billion in 2014. His professional achievements are but a small part of his story. He grew up in Kildare, one of five children raised by their mother, Peggy McCarthy MacIntyre, from Butte, Montana. His father is the well-known Irish playwright and poet Tom MacIntyre. Des is an active supporter of the American Ireland Fund in Boston and was the chairman of the 2013 Gala, which brought in more than $2.3 million. He is very involved in multiple charities and has been a strong advocate for the Alzheimer's Association. He is an avid sports fan and competitor in marathons, Ironman events and triathlons. In 2014, Des completed a swim from the Statue of Liberty past Ellis Island to the Morris Canal—an event that resonated with his Irish heritage. That adventure was topped by his summiting Mount Kilimanjaro.

Patrick F. Cadigan

Patrick F. Cadigan always finds a way to publicly sing *Danny Boy* when he returns to his alma mater, Boston College High School, just as he did at the dedication of Cadigan Hall, a $12 million building given by Pat to the all-male, Jesuit-run school in Dorchester. (Pat is shown here at the dedication.) Raised in Belmont by Irish-born parents, Pat attended Boston College High and Boston College. "I'm indebted to all of my schools," Pat told *The Orange County Register*. "They were all very good experiences, and I wish I could repeat them." He received advanced degrees from Boston University and Harvard and a doctorate from Claremont Graduate University. Pat is the former CEO and president of Electronic Engineering Co. of California and resides in Southern California. "My parents were not able to obtain a formal education," he said, "so I felt a very personal responsibility to give back to the wonderful schools that educated and shaped me."

Brian O'Donovan

Brian O'Donovan has worn a lot of hats since arriving in the United States in 1976 as part of a work-exchange program, but he is best known throughout the region for his three-hour weekly program, *A Celtic Sojourn*, which has aired on WGBH-FM since 1986. Brian has worked in event management in entertainment and sports. He was part of the team that brought the 1994 World Cup to the United States, overseeing the Boston games. Brian was involved in the founding of Major League Soccer in 1996 and became the

first general manager and COO of the New England Revolution of Major League Soccer. Born in the small seaside town of Clonakilty in West Cork, Brian graduated from University College Cork and emigrated permanently in 1980. One of his projects, the popular *Christmas Celtic Sojourn* series of concerts, which has been running for 12 years, played to more than 11,000 people in December 2013.

Arthur P. Boyle

Arthur P. Boyle knows that even the most faithful Catholic might have a hard time believing his life's story. In 1999, he was diagnosed with kidney cancer that had spread to his lungs. At the urging of friends Rob Griffin and Kevin Gill, Artie went to Medjugorje, Bosnia-Herzegovina, an apparition site of the Blessed Virgin Mary. It was there that Artie believes he was healed, and he chronicles his experiences in his 2014 book *Six Months to Live*. A development officer with the Archdiocese of Boston, he previously owned and operated a transportation business for 30 years. Artie's family came to Dorchester via Canada and traces its roots back to Galway. He and his wife, Judy, also an Irish American, have 13 children. Artie can rattle off something special about each of his children, but here are some highlights: The oldest, Jennifer, is a doctor and the mother of eight; the second born, Artie Jr., is autistic; the third in line, Michelle, a successful real estate broker, also has eight children; Brian plays hockey for the Tampa Bay Lightning; younger brother Tim was drafted by the Ottawa Senators; Chris is in the seminary; and Kathryn is working for the archdiocesan Office for the New Evangelization.

Thomas J. Hynes, Jr. and Thomas (Tod) J. Hynes, III

Thomas (Tom) J. Hynes, Jr. made a career in the real estate business at the urging of his uncle, Mayor John B. Hynes, who said that Boston had a great future, and Tom should play a role in its success and development. Tom is cochairman and CEO of Colliers International-Boston (formerly Meredith & Grew) and has been part of the evolving success of Boston for several decades. That drive is something that has been passed on to his son, **Thomas (Tod) J. Hynes, III**, founder and president of XL Hybrids, a company that makes battery electric hybrid powertrains for commercial vehicles. Tod is also a senior lecturer at Massachusetts Institute of Technology, where he teaches a graduate level course called Energy Ventures. The family is active in civic endeavors. Tom has served on a number of boards both of public companies, educational and nonprofit organizations. Tod cofounded the MIT Clean Energy Prize that has helped teams from more than 50 universities launch new energy ventures. The family's roots are as deep in Ireland as they are in Boston. Bernard Hynes, Tom's grandfather, came to Boston from Galway in 1888 as a young boy. Bernard worked in the Back Bay rail yards that eventually became the site of the Prudential Center—brought to Boston by his son, Mayor Hynes. Tom's Irish tradition is close to his heart as a member of the Charitable Irish Society, The Clover Club and the Eire Society. Tod played football, hockey, and lacrosse at MIT.

Jake Kennedy

Jake Kennedy began celebrating his Irish roots at age five, when his namesake was elected as the first Irish-Catholic U.S. president. Although he bears no relation to those Kennedys, Jake's family has made its own mark on Boston. One grandfather was president of Boston State Teachers College and the other was a Boston Police sergeant. Jake's father was dean of students and vice president at Northeastern, and Jake's mother raised eight children and was a special education teacher. Jake and his brother Rich created Kennedy Brothers Physical Therapy in the late 1980s and now manage six clinics; both continue to work full-time as physical therapists. In 1989, Jake and his wife, Sparky, created "Christmas in the City," an all-volunteer effort to give the city's homeless children their own holiday celebration. That first year, the party was held for 165 children living in shelters. In 2013, 4,400 homeless children were transported from around the region for a daylong celebration including food, entertainment, games, and gifts from their own wish lists. Another 10,000 children received gifts the following day.

With **Amy E. Ryan**'s appointment as president of the Boston Public Library, she became the first woman to hold the post in the library's 166-year history, overseeing one of the most comprehensive library systems in the country. Amy was named president in October 2008, after more than 30 years in the Minneapolis libraries. A Minnesota native, Amy's Irish-Catholic family was a rarity in White Bear Lake, Minnesota. Her father, John Paul Ryan, would talk about his father being a police officer in Newton. "My mother's father was an early employee at Gillette Company," Amy says. Her father has roots in Co. Tipperary; her mother, Anne Elizabeth (Hickey) Ryan's family hails from Co. Armagh in Northern Ireland. "I credit my parents for imbuing me with their commitment to curious thinking, reading, learning, telling stories, and seeking out new ideas," Amy says, "but most of all for their Irish wit and wisdom."

John Joyce

John Joyce is keeping a part of Ireland's history alive on the ponds and waterways of Boston. Johnny is shown with a model of a *curragh*, a boat used on Ireland's West Coast. Some 50 years ago, Johnny cofounded the Boston Irish Rowing Club with other area Irish Americans to build curraghs and hold races in Boston. Their efforts spread to other parts of the country. His family also holds a special place in Irish history. One of 11 children, Johnny's ancestor Patrick Joyce was the first to settle on the island of Innisbarra off the coast of Connemara. The families on the island used curraghs to get to the mainland. Johnny's late brother Máirtín Seoighe, whose story was documented in the 2001 book *Singing Shores, Whispering Wind: Voices of Connemara*, was the last inhabitant of the island. Sponsored by an aunt, Johnny immigrated to Boston and found work as a pressman at *The Boston Globe*, where his two sons, John Jr. and David, also work as pressmen.

L Street Brownies Swimming Club

More than 600 swimmers, some with elaborate costumes and others in skimpy bathing suits, braved the bitter New Year's Day air to take the 111th Annual Polar Bear Plunge into a frigid Dorchester Bay. Sponsored by the renowned **L Street Brownies Swimming Club**, the 2014 dip into the icy water was dedicated to noted election attorney **William A. McDermott, Jr.**, who was struck and killed by a car while crossing Day Boulevard at L Street in South Boston in February 2013. He was 67 when he died; in his obituary, *The Boston Globe* called him "a quintessentially Boston Irish character." He was also an L Street Brownie, and worked out at the bathhouse gym regularly. Billy never forgot his childhood in Savin Hill, growing up in a political family. He worked on dozens of campaigns supporting Democrats from the city to the national levels. Billy worked for the city during the White administration, and it was said that the only things in his life that ranked higher than politics were "Boston College hockey and his family."

James Hooley

Before being named Chief of Department in 2010, **James Hooley** had worked in just about every job at the City of Boston's Emergency Medical Services department—EMT, paramedic, shift commander, Superintendent of Field Operations, and Superintendent in Chief. Jim oversees a department that has more than 350 EMTs and paramedics who respond to an average of 300 emergencies per day—more than 116,000 per year, according to city records. When the two bombings that killed three and injured hundreds occurred near the finish line of the Boston Marathon in 2013, Jim's department was praised for clearing all the victims off the street in less than 20 minutes. A lifelong Boston resident, Jim and his five younger siblings were raised in Uphams Corner, where his family settled after emigrating from Co. Cork. A father of three, Jim has had two sons work in public safety: one son in the Boston Police Department and another in Boston EMS. Jim attended University of Massachusetts Boston and Harvard's John F. Kennedy School of Government.

Michael Joseph Donovan

Now in his seventh term as Clerk of the Suffolk County Superior Court, **Michael Joseph Donovan** (at the lectern) is the only person in the history of the Suffolk court to start at entry level and work in every position in the clerk's office. He was later appointed as assistant clerk of court and, in 1976, was elected Clerk of Court, the youngest person to hold the position. Raised in the Irish neighborhoods of Savin Hill and South Boston, Mike's paternal grandparents were from Co. Cork. Mike says that two of the most important events in his life occurred within two weeks of each other. In January 2014, Mike helped with the funeral arrangements of his friend and mentor former

state Attorney General Robert Quinn. Ten days earlier, his longtime friend Mayor Walsh asked Mike to speak at the inauguration. Behind Mike on the stage at Boston College's Conte Forum is the Boston City Council, six of whose members are Irish-American. They are (from left) councilors at large: **Michael Flaherty, Stephen Murphy, Ayanna Pressley,** and **Michelle Wu;** and district councilors: **Salvatore LaMattina, Bill Linehan, Frank Baker, Charles C. Yancy, Timothy McCarthy, Matt O'Malley, Tito Jackson, Josh Zakim,** and **Mark Ciommo.**

Peter O'Kane

Peter O'Kane never set out to own a semiprofessional football team. "It was the last thing I wanted to do," he says. But Pete and his wife, Marge, have owned the Randolph Oilers of the American Football Association for nearly 40 years. Pete played football as a lineman and later as a running back, first in high school and then for the Oilers. An injury cut his playing career short, and he ultimately became the owner and general manager of the South Shore team. Pete's father, James P. O'Kane, was born in Glasgow, Scotland, to Irish parents and immigrated to the United States, settling in Randolph. After working for the Randolph Police, James took a job in the newspaper distribution business and bought the company that delivered newspapers in the area. Pete worked with his father and notes that he is the first in his family to be able to retire. Not that he's taking it easy. "For the game last weekend," Pete said, "my job was to keep the footballs warm and dry."

Rob Griffin

Rob Griffin, president of the New England area for the commercial real estate firm Cushman & Wakefield, credits his mother, Frances, with instilling a sense of history and pride in his Irish heritage. "It wasn't that it was any one thing," Rob says, "it was everything from politics to President Kennedy to work ethic." A graduate of Boston College's Carroll School of Management, Rob is chairman of the Real Estate & Finance Council at Boston College and is a member of the Greater Boston Real Estate Board. Rob is on the board of Boston Children's Hospital and says that philanthropy is something he and his wife, Cathy, have tried to do as a family. Growing up in Scituate, Rob says his family was also engaged in that other Irish-American pastime—sports. "We played hockey and baseball all the time," Rob says. Rob's oldest son, Corey, 27, who played hockey while at Boston College, died in an August 2014 accident on Nantucket shortly after he had raised $100,000 for research into amyotrophic lateral sclerosis on behalf of his college friend Pete Frates, who has Lou Gehrig's disease.

Margery Eagan

Longtime newspaper columnist and radio talk show host **Margery Eagan** speaks up for people whose own voices aren't often heard. After 27 years as a reporter and columnist for the *Boston Herald*, Margery joined *The Boston Globe* in July 2014 as a columnist for its Catholicism-news website, Crux. Margery and Jim Braude host *Boston Public Radio*, a three-hour weekday issues talk show on WGBH-FM. Margery grew up in Fall River and graduated from Stanford University. She remembers her father and grandfather going to Boston every year in tuxedos for the Clover Club's St. Patrick's Day party. On her mother's side, the Irish pride shone bright. Her maternal grandmother, Lillian Kiley, was not yet 13 years old when she traveled by herself to Massachusetts from Co. Waterford. Lillian met and married Bill Manning, who left Co. Cork for America and built a successful auto supply business.

Peggy Dray

Peggy Dray's career in creating and managing events started when her friend Kevin White decided to run for Secretary of the Commonwealth of Massachusetts. "He asked me to organize social events throughout the state where he could meet and greet voters," Peggy says. "Kevin won the election." When White ran for mayor, Peggy and a friend organized teas and events in all of Boston's wards and later planned the inaugural ball. Peggy was a cofounder of Daisy Associates, which, among other big events, opened the Stadium Club at the old Foxboro Stadium. She then worked for the Boston Park Plaza Hotel for 20 years and is now with The Fairmont Copley Plaza hotel. Peggy's ancestors emigrated from Connemara, Co. Cork and Co. Mayo to Boston. At age 15, her grandfather D.W. Dunn started his own moving and storage company after his parents died suddenly. Peggy notes, with a hint of pride, that the business became very successful.

Margaret Stapleton

While volunteering at the Pine Street Inn, **Margaret Stapleton** saw that the South End shelter could do more to provide permanent housing for some of the chronically homeless people whom it served. That led her to make a donation that created Stapleton House, an 11-resident home on Harrison Avenue in the South End that provides housing and programs for the men in residence. A retired senior managing director and vice president with John Hancock Financial Services, Margaret first got involved with the Pine Street Inn through her church, St. Mary of the Nativity in Scituate, and has been involved with the nonprofit for more than 25 years. Margaret was born in Ireland and emigrated when she was 19. She is on the board of the Irish Pastoral Care Centre and is a member and past president of the Eire Society of Boston.

Michael Sherlock and John Joe Somers

After doing a three-year stint at University College, London, **Michael Sherlock**, (left), who hails from Athenry, Co. Galway, decided to find greener pastures and immigrated to United States. After arriving in Boston, Michael worked at a succession of small companies until 1976, when he became general manager of the now famous Black Rose pub on State Street. Despite the fact that Quincy Market was still undergoing its transformation into a tourist destination, the "Rose," as it was commonly called, became a sensation. Once called "a bar of character with characters" by *Time* magazine, The Black Rose was featured on late-night national television on *The Tomorrow Show* with Tom Snyder, garnering some 11 million viewers. Michael went on to create and manage new locations such as The Midnight Court and Limericks, eventually meeting with the ultimate bar/restaurant entrepreneur **John Joe Somers**, who was then looking to open an Irish-themed restaurant. After numerous searches—and many more field trips—for possible locations, John finally settled on a location on Broad Street in the Financial District. After a major overhaul, Mr. Dooley's was born. Named after the great Chicago journalist Peter Finley Dunne, who wrote a series of pieces in the late 19th century as "Mr. Dooley," the establishment quickly gained a great name for itself, drawing visitors from all walks of life including dignitaries from the political and entertainment arenas. John went on to open the Green Dragon, Hennessy's, Paddio's and Dirty Nelly's, all in the vicinity of Boston City Hall. John, who hails from Co. Kerry, is an accomplished guitarist and singer.

David Greaney

As founder and president of the real estate development and investment company Synergy Investments, **David Greaney** has overseen his firm's growth into a powerful presence in the Boston area. Under Dave's tenure, Synergy Investments owns and operates more than 30 buildings that house more than 375 companies in approximately 3 million square feet. Before starting Synergy, Dave held investment management groups of Harvard University and PricewaterhouseCoopers. Born in Limerick and a graduate of University College Dublin, Dave continues to give back to the region's Irish-American community. He received recognition from The Boston Irish Business Association, the Irish Chamber of Commerce, *Irish America* magazine and the Irish magazine *Business & Finance*. Dave actively supports a number of charitable causes, including the American Ireland Fund and the Claddagh Fund, the charitable foundation of the Dropkick Murphys.

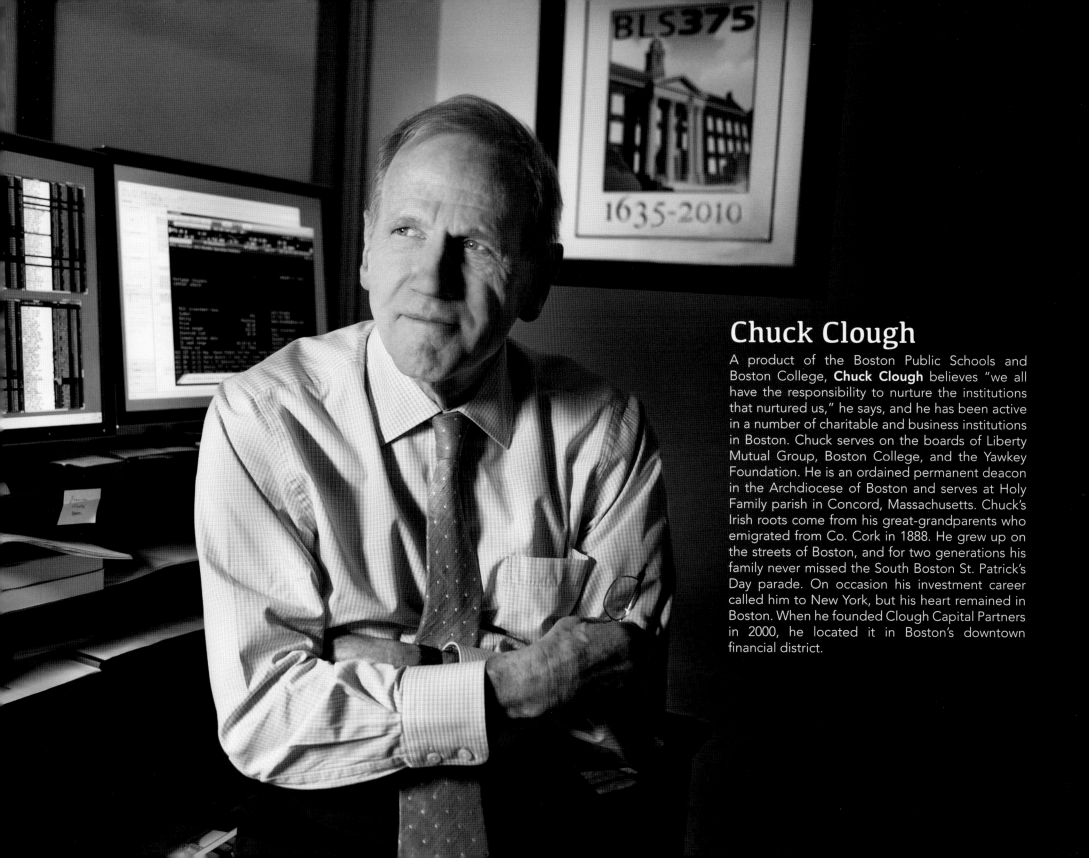

Chuck Clough

A product of the Boston Public Schools and Boston College, **Chuck Clough** believes "we all have the responsibility to nurture the institutions that nurtured us," he says, and he has been active in a number of charitable and business institutions in Boston. Chuck serves on the boards of Liberty Mutual Group, Boston College, and the Yawkey Foundation. He is an ordained permanent deacon in the Archdiocese of Boston and serves at Holy Family parish in Concord, Massachusetts. Chuck's Irish roots come from his great-grandparents who emigrated from Co. Cork in 1888. He grew up on the streets of Boston, and for two generations his family never missed the South Boston St. Patrick's Day parade. On occasion his investment career called him to New York, but his heart remained in Boston. When he founded Clough Capital Partners in 2000, he located it in Boston's downtown financial district.

Michael G. Conlon, Jr.

When **Michael G. Conlon, Jr**. took ownership of the Stockyard restaurant in Brighton in 2012, many in the local community were relieved to know the landmark steakhouse was in good hands. Michael and his two siblings were raised nearby in Brighton in St. Columbkille's Parish by their parents, Mike, who emigrated from Swinford, Co. Mayo, and Mary (O'Rourke), from Athlone, Co. Roscommon. Michael learned the business from his father, who opened the Blarney Stone with a couple of partners in 1965.

The Fields Corner bar and restaurant made history when it was awarded the exclusive license to serve Guinness in Boston. Fans of the popular Irish stout included the late Boston Pops maestro Arthur Fielder. Michael, whose father did not want him to go into the restaurant business, sold the Blarney Stone in 2013. Still, he now owns five other eateries, including the Paramount on Beacon Hill and South Boston, West on Centre in West Roxbury, and Lincoln in South Boston.

Barbara Clement Reilly

The youngest of four, **Barbara Clement Reilly** grew up in Westwood, started college at American University, but returned to Boston after a year so that she could work to pay her way through Northeastern University's night program. That's when Barbara started in the advertising business and, after working at several agencies, she joined Arnold Worldwide, where she is now managing partner and executive director. A key part of her role at Arnold is the firm's pro bono and charitable initiative "Arnold Gives Back," which includes the House of Possibilities and the American Heart Association's "Go Red For Women" campaign. A mother of two daughters, Barbara's Irish ancestry traces back primarily to Co. Leitrim, while others lived in Cavan, Donegal, Dublin, and Kildare counties. She has been married to Mark Reilly, also from a large Boston family, for nearly 30 years. His father, John Reilly, worked for the Red Sox as the organization's treasurer from 1946 until his retirement in 1992.

Brian McGrory

As 2012 came to a close, *The Boston Globe* announced that **Brian McGrory**, a Metro columnist who once delivered *The Globe* as a paperboy, would be its next editor. Brian grew up in Roslindale and Weymouth and graduated from Bates College. He worked at *The New Haven Register* and *The Patriot Ledger* before joining *The Globe* in 1989. Brian's first trip to Ireland was as a reporter covering Cardinal Bernard F. Law and Mayor Ray Flynn "for a whirlwind tour of Belfast." Brian also reported on President Clinton's historic trip to Ireland. *The Globe* newsroom was tested early on in Brian's tenure when two bombs went off at the finish line of the 2013 Boston Marathon, killing three and wounding more than 260. The newspaper and its websites were awarded the 2014 Pulitzer Prize for breaking news. When the awards were announced, Brian told the newsroom that he was proud of their work but took no joy in covering the story.

Ronan Noonan

Irish-born playwright **Ronan Noone** has seen his plays performed on stages in Boston, New York, London, Edinburgh, Los Angeles, Chicago, and Washington, D.C., and at the Williamstown Theatre Festival, yet "never in Ireland," he says. "But you'll have that." Ronan left his hometown of Clifden, Co. Galway, for Martha's Vineyard, where he worked as a bartender before becoming a student in Boston University's playwriting program where he now teaches. Ronan, a U.S. citizen, has penned several plays, including the award-winning trilogy: *The Lepers of Baile Baiste, The Blowin of Baile Gall*, and *The Gigolo of Baile Breag.* Ronan got his start with the Boston Playwrights' Theatre and the former Súgán Theatre Company, which is why Boston's theater community proudly claims him. His latest play, *The Second Girl*, is on the Huntington Theatre Company's 2015 schedule. Kevin Cullen described Ronan in a 2009 *Boston Globe* profile as occupying "that space, the hyphen, between Irish and American, mining the inherent contradictions of those two, often clashing cultures for laughs and pathos."

Martin Richard Vigil

On April 16, 2013, just a little more than a day after two bombs exploded near the Boston Marathon finish line, five thousand people gathered and held candles at Garvey Park in Dorchester to remember eight-year-old Martin Richard, the youngest of the three victims. The moving event was more spontaneous than planned, say the community leaders who were among those at the park where Martin had often played with friends. Remembered by family and friends as a happy third-grade student who liked to run and jump, Martin was with his family when the blasts went off. Also killed on Patriots Day were Krystle Campbell, 29, of Medford, and Lu Lingzi, a 23-year-old graduate student from China. A fourth person, MIT police Officer Sean Collier, 27, was allegedly killed by the bombing suspects three days later.

James Callanan

James Callanan will tell you proudly that he is a lifelong, third-generation South Boston resident whose family emigrated from Co. Cork more than a century ago. The owner of Boston–based event production company JCALPRO, Jimmy has worked in the entertainment infrastructure industry for more than 30 years. He has worked with the Boston Symphony Orchestra and Boston Ballet and in a variety of venues such as Symphony Hall, Boston Garden and Gillette Stadium. His work includes films like *The* *Perfect Storm*, *Good Will Hunting*, *Mermaids,* and *The Witches of Eastwick*; and TV shows like *Spenser: For Hire*. Jimmy's work often involves travel and he has visited more than 30 countries, including his favorite: Ireland. He sits on many community nonprofit boards and established the nonprofit South Boston Scholarship for the Arts. He helps produce the annually televised St. Patrick's Day Breakfast in Boston.

Denis Keohane

Born and raised in Kinsale, Co. Cork, **Denis Keohane** came to the United States in 1988 at the age of 21, and he says he immediately set out to make his mark in real estate investment and development in the Boston area. A Milton resident for more than 20 years, Denis then pursued that other Irish passion: politics. He was the first foreign-born elected member of the Milton School Committee in 2010, and two years later he became the first foreign-born elected member of the Milton Board of Selectmen, serving as board chair in 2013-2014. Denis and his wife, Mary, a fifth-generation Irish American, have three daughters. Denis has been recognized for his work in the Irish community and was given the "member of year" award by the Friendly Sons of Saint Patrick, a New Bedford–based nonprofit that works to preserve Irish culture while supporting area social service

The Ridge Family

Family patriarch **Gerald M. Ridge** stands at the center of his four nephews—all members of the Boston Police Department. They are, from left, Patrolman **John M. Ridge**, Sergeant **Robert J. Ridge**, Deputy Superintendent **William G. Ridge**, and Detective **Stephen J. Ridge**. The men are the sons of Gerry's brother, William J. Ridge, a Boston Police detective with 30 years on the job who died in 1988 while on active duty. The Ridges emigrated from Connemara and came to America in the late 19th century by way of Portland, Maine. They moved to Boston in the early 20th century, ultimately settling in South Boston's lower end. Gerry was also a former Boston Police Patrolman who left the job in the early 1960s. A successful businessman, Gerry is best known for his many years running the Blue Hill Cemetery. In 1985, Gerry founded and built the Boston Police Athletic League as a community crime prevention resource. It was the first police athletic league in the state. He has been an adviser and supporter of Cops for Kids with Cancer and other programs that support education and athletics.

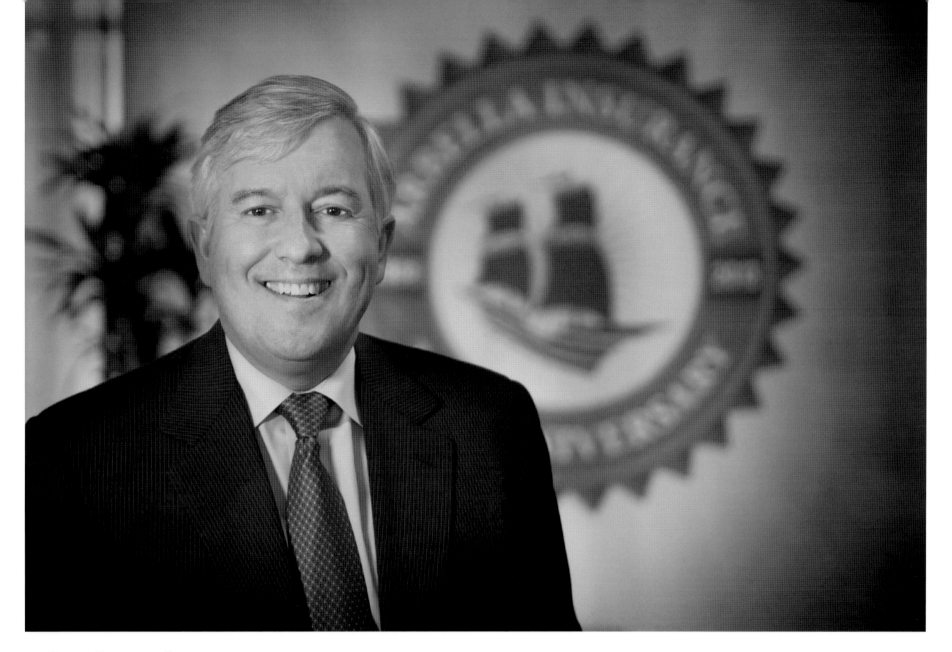

John Donohue

Family man, father of three grown sons, and president and CEO of the Arbella Insurance Group, **John Donohue** is proud of his Irish heritage, which traces back to Co. Armagh and Ballyporeen, Co. Tipperary. His grandparents Rose (Morgan) and Jeffrey Donohue made their home in Danbury, Connecticut, where he worked as a porter on the local railroad. The couple did well enough that John's father, John F. Donohue, graduated from Yale in 1948, the first in the family to earn a college diploma. John says his passion to support immigration reform comes directly from his family's history. For more than 10 years, he has worked closely with the Irish International Immigrant Center in Boston, where he has served as chair of its advisory board, helping to raise funds, jobs, awareness and support not only for the Irish but for all immigrants entering the United States. A resident of Belmont for more than 25 years, John had not visited Ireland until 2014, when he and his family spent time there with his son, who was attending college in Dublin.

Mary Walsh

As proud as she is of her children, **Mary Walsh**, mother of Mayor Martin J. Walsh, isn't one to seek the spotlight. Mary, who was born in the Connemara region on Ireland's West coast, still lives in the three-decker on Taft Street where she and her late husband, John, raised their two sons, Johnny and Marty. It is also where she was photographed. Mary (O'Malley) immigrated to America in 1959, and John came from the nearby Callowfeenish, Carna, Co. Galway, just a couple of years before her. The couple, like so many others in the area, met at a dance at Intercolonial Hall in Roxbury's Dudley Square. John worked for 50 years as part of the Laborers Union, Local 223, where his son Marty also worked for a number of years, and passed away on June 2, 2010, at age 82. Mary traveled with Marty in September 2014 back to Ireland on his first visit since he was elected mayor. The tour, which included stops at the family's house in Rosmuc and appearances on late-night television, was like a second inauguration,

Frank McLaughlin

As an adult, **Frank McLaughlin**, the always curious, hardworking Boston College economics professor, developed an interest in the Irish language. He and his brother Reverend John McLaughlin joined the Cumann Na Gaeilge, an Irish language and culture society, and solidified the connection from his grandparents to his grandchildren. Frank is the second of eight children to Nora and Francis McLaughlin. He grew up in St. Patrick's Parish in Roxbury, graduated from Roxbury Memorial High School and has lived his entire life in the city of Boston. He is the first person on either side of his family to graduate from high school, and he then went on to earn three degrees in economics—a bachelor's and master's at Boston College, and a doctorate at Massachusetts Institute of Technology's Sloan School of Management. He married Clare (Carr) in 1954. They have 11 children and 27 grandchildren and one great-grandchild. When Frank retired from Boston College after 54 years of teaching, he had shaped the lives of some 25,000 students.

Aidan Browne

Although **Aidan Browne** will tell you that one of the proudest moments of his life was becoming an American citizen in 1999, he remains Irish to the core, having grown up the youngest of seven children on the north side of Dublin. It was love at first sight when he visited America as a 17-year-old college student and returned two years later to work in Burlington, Vermont. Love struck again when he met his wife, Jill, while they were both working at the Sheraton Burlington hotel. After qualifying as a lawyer and practicing in Dublin, he and Jill came to Boston in 1986 with their young

family—Jessica and Sam; a third child, Caoimhe, came along later. Now a partner at the Boston firm of Sullivan & Worcester, Aidan has worked in investment between Ireland and the United States, has hosted many leading Irish business and political leaders in Boston, and has worked with several Irish charities over the years. Aidan, who splits his time between South Boston and Vermont, counts winning the 2006 "World Father and Son" Golf Tournament at Waterville Golf Club in Ireland among his greatest memories.

Patricia Maguire Meservey

From Salem State University President **Patricia Maguire Meservey**'s office you can hear the sounds of construction being done on campus and the students going to and from class. "I like being near the students and the bustle of the campus," Pat says. As the 13th president of the university, Pat was instrumental in acquiring university status for Salem State in 2010. Each St. Patrick's Day, Pat leads a contingent from the university in the Naples, Florida, parade. She came to Salem State in 2007 from Suffolk University, where she was the first provost and academic vice president. Previously, she held positions at Northeastern University and Boston University. Trained as a nurse, Pat has a master's degree in parent-child health from Boston University and a doctorate in higher education administration from Boston College. Growing up in Framingham, Pat recalls hearing stories from her maternal grandmother, Celia, who had emigrated at age 18 from Co. Cavan. "She lived with us for about 10 years, and it was a special experience having my grandmother tell us about her life," Pat says.

Michael Joyce

Michael Joyce has enjoyed great success in his career in commercial real estate, but it is the work that he and his wife, Jane, have done to help raise more than $6 million to fund research for Rett syndrome that makes him most proud. Mike, a partner at Transwestern, became involved with the International Rett Syndrome Foundation when Caroline, the second of their three daughters, was diagnosed with the often-debilitating neurological disorder that affects primarily girls. Mike cofounded Richards Barry Joyce & Partners, a commercial real estate company in Boston, in 2001. He and his partners sold the company to Transwestern in 2013. His grandparents came to America from Connemara and lived in Dorchester before heading out to Wilbraham, Massachusetts. It was his parents' hard work to put him and his siblings through college that taught him the importance of family support. "If they can do that, I can do anything," Mike says.

Jay Calnan

After graduating from Tufts, where he was a captain of the championship football team, **Jay Calnan** got his start in construction working on the "Big Dig" for Modern Continental and the late Les Marino. A short time later, he cashed out his 401(k) and started his company, J. Calnan & Associates, with just a desk and a phone. His company is now one of New England's leading construction management firms and has been recognized as one of the *Boston Business Journal*'s "Most Philanthropic Corporate Companies" for eight years in a row. He is a cofounder of Team IMPACT, a national nonprofit organization that improves the quality of life for children with life-threatening illnesses by "drafting" them onto college athletic teams. His ancestors immigrated to the United States during the Famine through St. John's, New Brunswick. "A strong work ethic, resilience, and never-give-up attitude were instilled in me by my parents growing up in Bristol, Connecticut," Jay says. "I have tried to pass that on to my children—Christopher, Daintry, and Jake."

Mayor Joseph C. Sullivan

A lifelong resident of Braintree, Mayor **Joseph C. Sullivan II** knows and loves his town. Prior to becoming mayor in 2008, Joe served as state representative from 1993 to 2003, where he made the Old Colony Rail Lines service for the South Shore his priority, and he was the youngest person elected to the Braintree Board of Selectmen. Joe also was the executive director of the Massachusetts State Lottery for four years. He graduated from the University of Massachusetts Amherst and received a master's degree in public administration from Harvard's John F. Kennedy School of Government. His family came from Carna in the Connemara region to Braintree, fitting given that nearly 36 percent of his town claims Irish heritage, according to U.S. Census records. "My Irish heritage has taught me that the importance of a good sense of humor—as we travel through life—is a strong Irish trait that should be emulated," he says.

John T. Carroll

Some of Carroll Advertising President **John T. Carroll**'s best memories, he says, come from when he was seven years old. "We spent the whole summer in Ireland, and it was magical," John says. Both of his parents came to America from the Connemara region of Co. Galway; his father, Thomas M. Carroll, was born in Ballyconneely and his mother, Nora R. (McDonough), in neighboring Calla, Roundstone. Like so many others, Thomas found work as a laborer out of Local 223 in Dorchester—and

John would join him in the union during and after college. Nora worked full-time cleaning houses while raising John and his four sisters. He says that there was always music in his childhood home in Norwood. John got started in the advertising business by selling ads for the *Dorchester Reporter*. He later worked selling billboard space and in 1996 he started his own company and witnessed the changes from hand-painted signs to new digital ones.

Joe Fallon

The development of the South Boston waterfront as a thriving new hub of the city seems so obvious in 2014, but, just 10 years earlier, there were many who thought **Joe Fallon** was taking a huge risk in trying to build where others had failed. Joe's Fan Pier project—located between the John Joseph Moakley Federal Courthouse and the Institute of Contemporary Art—is already home to high-rise office towers, luxury residences, restaurants and retail space, including the clothier, Louis Boston. More high-profile restaurants and a marina are planned. Joe was photographed outside one of the office buildings at One Marina Park Drive at the front

of the Fan Pier project. He says he was always being trained for his life as a developer; he learned about the construction business from his father and counts the late Boston real estate icon Tom Flatley as a mentor. Joe started The Fallon Company in 1993 and has been part of several of the city's biggest developments. Joe, who traces his family's lineage back to Co. Galway, has supported numerous nonprofit organizations including WGBH, The Boston Symphony Orchestra, and Beth Israel Deaconess Medical Center.

Dr. James O'Connell

Despite aspirations of a career in oncology after finishing his residency in medicine at Massachusetts General Hospital, Dr. **James O'Connell** was recruited in 1985 by Dr. Thomas Durant to be the full-time doctor for a new citywide program to care for homeless individuals and families in Boston. The Boston Health Care for the Homeless Program has grown to be the largest and most comprehensive in the country, with teams of doctors, nurses and social workers providing direct care in more than 70 shelters and soup kitchens in Greater Boston, as well as daily clinics at Boston Medical Center and M.G.H. He graduated from the University of Notre Dame, studied theology at Cambridge University from 1970-72, taught high school and coached basketball at St. Louis High School in Honolulu, worked in restaurants, traveled, and skied with old friends in Northern Vermont before going to Harvard Medical School at the age of 30. Jim is an assistant professor of medicine at Harvard Medical School and MGH, where he is training the next generation of doctors to carry on his work.

Bob Reynolds

The CEO of Great-West Financial and Putnam Investments, **Bob Reynolds** was raised in West Virginia and came to Boston in the 1980s. At Fidelity Investments in Boston, he rose through the executive ranks to become the firm's chief operating officer. Bob helped to create America's workplace savings system while increasing Fidelity's 401(k) assets from $3 billion to more than $600 billion over his years at the firm. Named to head Putnam Investments in 2008, Bob led that firm to the number two position among 55 mutual fund families in overall five-year investment performance. In 2014, he became president and CEO of Great-West Financial as well and is now shaping America's second-largest retirement services firm. Long a booster of many worthy organizations in his adopted city, Bob, who takes great pride in his family's roots in Co. Leitrim, is national director and chairman of the Boston advisory board of the American Ireland Fund. The Fund's work, he says, "has helped bring peace and hope to all of the people of Ireland."

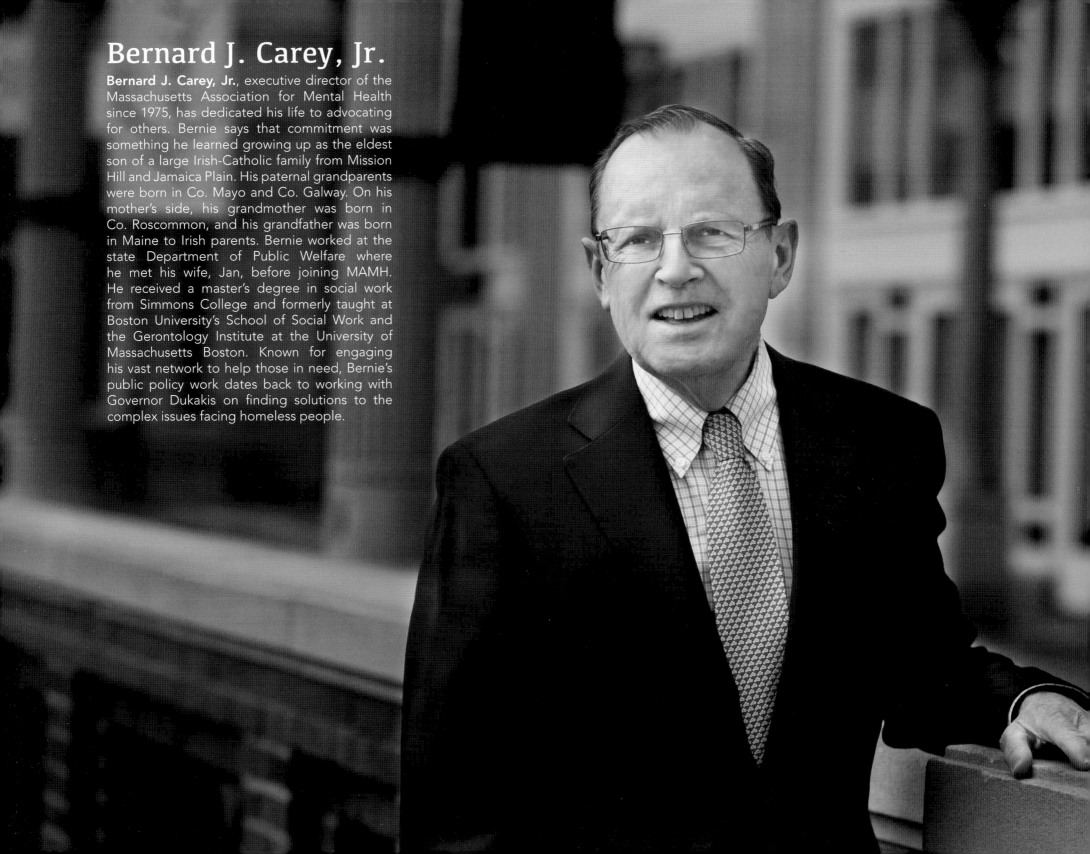

Bernard J. Carey, Jr.

Bernard J. Carey, Jr., executive director of the Massachusetts Association for Mental Health since 1975, has dedicated his life to advocating for others. Bernie says that commitment was something he learned growing up as the eldest son of a large Irish-Catholic family from Mission Hill and Jamaica Plain. His paternal grandparents were born in Co. Mayo and Co. Galway. On his mother's side, his grandmother was born in Co. Roscommon, and his grandfather was born in Maine to Irish parents. Bernie worked at the state Department of Public Welfare where he met his wife, Jan, before joining MAMH. He received a master's degree in social work from Simmons College and formerly taught at Boston University's School of Social Work and the Gerontology Institute at the University of Massachusetts Boston. Known for engaging his vast network to help those in need, Bernie's public policy work dates back to working with Governor Dukakis on finding solutions to the complex issues facing homeless people.

Thomas F. and Mark Shields

When **Thomas F. Shields**, (left), the founder of a diagnostic imaging and radiation therapy company, was honored by Tufts Medical Center with its inaugural Ellen M. Zane Award for Visionary Leadership, his brother **Mark Shields**, a Washington pundit and columnist, was on hand to celebrate at the March 7, 2014, event. One cannot tell the story of Tom and the Quincy–based Shields Health Care Group, without including his wife, Mary Jane (Murphy) Shields, who died on January 7, 2014, at age 84. The couple started the family-run business that now has 20 centers that offer outpatient MRI, radiation oncology, positron emission tomography, elder care and dialysis services. Tom, Mary Jane, and their seven children support a host of charities, often doing so quietly, including the Brain Science Foundation, Brockton Boys & Girls Club, Habitat for Humanity, and scholarship aid for students of Boston College, Boston College High School, Nativity Prep Boston, Trinity Catholic Academy, and Stonehill College, where the Science Center bears the name of Mary and Tom Shields. Tom and his brother Mark were raised in Weymouth. Mark attended the University of Notre Dame and enlisted in the U.S. Marine Corps. He worked on several campaigns including Mayor Kevin White's 1975 reelection campaign and Robert F. Kennedy's 1968 run the presidency. In 1979, Mark became an editorial writer for *The Washington Post* and began his nationally syndicated column. He also is a regular contributor to the *PBS NewsHour*. In one of his columns, Mark wrote: "To be fair, we Irish are not any day at the beach ourselves. It was the gifted Brendan Behan who wrote, 'Other people have a nationality; the Irish and the Jews have a psychosis.'"

William F. Kennedy

Although **William F. Kennedy** traces his family's Irish roots to Co. Wexford, his life is rooted in St. Peter's Parish in Dorchester. One of seven children born to Bill and Mary Kennedy, Bill grew up at a time when all activities, traditions, and friendships centered on parish life. He attended the College of the Holy Cross, where he remains active today, and credits the Jesuits for their leadership in serving others. For many years, he was chief of staff and chief legal counsel to Massachusetts Speaker of the House of Representatives Thomas M. Finneran. Bill is a prominent member of the Massachusetts Bar and a partner at the Boston firm of Nutter, McClennen & Fish. Bill is active in many causes and serves on many boards of major institutions, colleges and charities. Project Bread, Pope John Paul Academy, and the Children's Trust Fund are among the causes he supports. Bill is married to Annmarie Loeney, "a St. Mark's girl," as he describes her, and they have a daughter, Nora.

Peggy Nucci

Peggy Nucci says there is nothing she wanted to do more than to make a difference in the lives of young people in Boston, the city where she was raised and still calls home. Peggy retired in the summer of 2014 from the Boston Public Schools after a 35-year career. She has worked in schools in every neighborhood of the city, solving problems and providing counsel and, often, just plain love to hundreds of schoolchildren with serious disabilities or family problems. Peggy, who was never called Margaret to avoid being confused with her mother, was raised in St. Mark's Parish in Dorchester. Her parents' families hailed from Galway, and they frequently went back for visits. "My mother spoke Gaelic, loved the Irish arts, and had a career in sewing. She even invented her very own Aran Islands sweater pattern," Peggy said. Her parents were serious collectors of Waterford crystal and the house was full of special pieces of the hand-cut glass. "I remember having to be *very* careful walking around for fear of breaking anything."

Thomas Patrick Glynn III

As the Chief Executive Officer of the Massachusetts Port Authority **Thomas Patrick Glynn III** runs an organization that connects Boston and New England to the global economy. Tom's connection to Ireland goes well beyond the Aer Lingus flights from Boston Logan to Shannon and Dublin. His father's family settled in Jamaica Plain and his mother's family in Winchester. Both families were 100-percent Irish. His wife, Marylou Batt, also had a mother who was 100-percent Irish. It is no surprise that Tom and Marylou spent their honeymoon, fifth, and 30th anniversaries as visitors to Galway, Connemara, and Dublin. In 1988, Tom was proud to work with Mayor Ray Flynn, John Drew, and Steve Coyle to launch the first Irish Trade Festival at the World Trade Center Boston. Prior to his service at Massport Tom taught at the Harvard Kennedy School, served as chief operating officer at Partners HealthCare, deputy secretary of labor under President Bill Clinton, and general manager of the Massachusetts Bay Transportation Authority.

Kathleen Sullivan Meyer

Kathleen Sullivan Meyer, vice chair of the Massachusetts Board of Registration in Medicine, is the first person in her family to receive a law degree. "Education was the ticket out of poverty," says Kathy, "and my Irish family believed that there was no better education for an Irish-Catholic child than at the hands of the Jesuits and the Sisters of St. Joseph." Kathy's family is from the counties of Donegal and Cork. Her mother, Dorothy Gibbons Sullivan, was raised in Dorchester, and her father, John Sullivan, grew up in Charlestown, the son of a Beacon Hill mailman. They met while they were waiting for a bus on the Boston College campus where they were both studying chemistry. Most of Kathy's legal career was spent as an attorney and partner at the Boston law firm Lubin & Meyer. Thirty-two years ago, she married the firm's founding partner, Andrew C. Meyer, Jr.; they have three children—two are lawyers and one is in medical school.

Boston Fire Department Commissioners

Shortly before **Joseph E. Finn** (right) took the oath of office as the 42nd commissioner of the Boston Fire Department at the Engine 20 firehouse in Neponset, he caught up with three of his predecessors (from left) **Martin E. Pierce, Jr.**, **Paul A. Christian**, and **Leo D. Stapleton**. Joe picked the firehouse for the ceremony because it was where his father, Paul, worked and not far from where he grew up. Joe's family hails from Kiltoom, Co. Roscommon. A former Marine, Joe joined the department in 1984 (the same year that Leo was named commissioner) and steadily worked his way up through the ranks. In making the appointment, Mayor Walsh also named Joe chief of the department. Marty, who comes from a prominent family of firefighters, was named commissioner and chief of the department on January 3, 1991.

His grandparents emigrated from Co. Cork. The son of an ironworker, Paul was raised in the City Point section of South Boston, graduated from Boston Technical High School, and holds a master's degree in engineering from Northeastern University. He was named commissioner on November 9, 2001. Paul's grandmother emigrated from Dublin. A veteran of the U.S. Navy during World War II, Leo was a member of the department for 39 years. He was appointed as commissioner and chief of department on February 1, 1984, and served in that capacity for the last seven years of his career. His father, John V. Stapleton, was appointed chief of department in 1950; two of his sons, Leo Jr. and Garrett, joined the department in the 1970s. The Stapleton family traces its roots back to Co. Kerry.

Hank Brennan and J. W. Carney, Jr.

Hank Brennan (left) and **J. W. "Jay" Carney, Jr.** are two of the best and the best-known criminal defense attorneys in Boston. Hank's great-grandparents emigrated from Co. Cork and settled in Waltham, Massachusetts. Hank's father, Henry Brennan, Sr., was one of nine children. Hank says, "My parents instilled a depth of character and discipline in me that resulted in a tremendous work ethic." His father worked three jobs and raised his children in Natick, Massachusetts. Jay's paternal ancestors came from Co. Cork and Co. Kerry to settle in Fall River, Massachusetts. Jay says that his father worked long hours as his mother raised five children. "It was a household full of love, grand stories," he says, "and frequent get-togethers with dozens of cousins." Jay says that his best decision was to ask Joy Rosen to marry him 32 years ago, and they are the proud parents of Julia and Nat, "who always seek the road less traveled." Jay says his second-best decision was asking the trial attorney, Hank Brennan, to be his co-counsel after Jay was appointed to represent James "Whitey" Bulger in 2011 for his Federal racketeering trial. "But that's a whole other story," says Jay.

Christine M. Griffin

When a car accident left **Christine M. Griffin** with a permanent spinal cord injury and she needed a wheelchair to get around, it also gave her a new calling: disability rights law. After a three-year enlistment in the U.S. Army, Chris entered Massachusetts Maritime Academy, in the second class that included women, and graduated with a degree in marine engineering. She later attended Boston College Law School and has since had a two-decade career of public service working on disability rights law in Washington, D.C., and Boston. She is the executive director of the Disability Law Center. Her family's story starts in Co. Westmeath in the Irish midlands and includes Kilmarnock, Scotland, and Co. Antrim. Her great-grandparents Tom and Margaret (McCormack) Griffin emigrated from Kilkenny to Prince Edward Island. Her grandfather set out for Boston at age 20 seeking any work that didn't include farming; he became a baker. The family settled in Dorchester, where Chris and her six siblings were raised.

Daniel A. Mullin and Kevin J. Ahearn

Daniel A. Mullin (left) and **Kevin J. Ahearn** each have had extraordinary success in the city's exclusive real estate market. Dan and his agency are known for their bespoke projects, such as handling a single historically significant property, while Kevin's Otis & Ahearn has gained a national reputation for representing developers when large residential projects go online. The two were photographed on the famed Acorn Street in Beacon Hill, not far from where Dan has made his home for decades. For the Arlington–born and bred Dan, Beacon Hill holds a particular significance because his immigrant grandfather worked as a janitor for Brahmins there. Dan, who went to Boston College High School and Boston College, traces his family's roots to the counties of Cork and Clare. Dan is a founder of Good Samaritan Hospice and is on the board of the Fine Art Work Center in Provincetown. A Milton native, Kevin attended Milton High School but transferred to Catholic Memorial in his sophomore year because of the school's powerhouse hockey program. Kevin was awarded a hockey scholarship to Boston College, where he received a bachelor's degree in marketing. He played on the 1972 U.S. Winter Olympic hockey team that won a silver medal in Sapporo, Japan, leading the team in goals scored. He played professionally for three years before launching a real estate career. His ancestors emigrated from the Ireland counties of Waterford and Wexford.

Bob Scannell and Mary Kinsella Scannell

Don't tell **Bob Scannell**, president and CEO of the Boys & Girls Clubs of Dorchester, or his wife, **Mary Kinsella Scannell**, the Clubs' vice president, that there are young people in Boston who can't be helped and given a chance to learn in safe circumstances. Under Bob's 27 years of leadership, the Clubs' organization has grown from one building serving hundreds of children to an agency with three sites, all located in Dorchester, that serves more than 4,000 children. Mary joined her husband at BGCD 26 years ago and they, along with the staff, have created a place where children from two months to 18 years old can grow, learn and develop meaningful relationships through diverse programs. Bob, who has been called "Dot's

Mr. Dependable" by the *Dorchester Reporter*, is known for being tough but fair. He once put Mark Wahlberg on an "extended time-out" and now serves on the board of the actor's foundation. Mary and Bob are as proud of their Irish ancestry as they are of their Dorchester roots. Bob's great-grandparents were from Killorglin and his "bucket list" includes playing the historic golf courses there in Co. Kerry. Both sets of Mary's grandparents were from Ireland. Her paternal grandparents emigrated from Tipperary and Cork. Her maternal grandparents were both raised in Co. Galway in the villages of Bealadangan and Rosmuc.

Máirín Uí Chéide-Keady

Máirín Uí Chéide-Keady was born and raised on the West Coast of Ireland in Lettermore, a little village known the world over thanks to the song *Peigín Leitir Móir*. This region known as Gorumna Islands, or Ceantar na nOileán, is a stronghold of the Irish language. Máirín, a native fluent speaker, is an acclaimed Seannós singer who immigrated to Boston in 1986 and was discovered by Larry Reynolds, the renowned fiddler and dean of Irish music in the region. She won the prestigious Corn Uí Riada competition and has performed throughout the United States and Canada. She has sung for President Bill Clinton and presidents of Ireland, including Mary Robinson, Mary McAleese, and Michael D. Higgins. She is a regular correspondent for RTÉ Raidió na Gaeltachta. Now an American citizen, this mother of five (one of whom served as a sergeant in the U.S. Army's 82nd Airborne Division) is actively involved with Mass Fallen Heroes in South Boston.

George F. Gilpin

George F. Gilpin, a lifelong Dorchester resident, is a cofounder of EasCare Ambulance Service. From its Dorchester headquarters, EasCare employs more than 550 full- and part-time employees working on 150 vehicles at 11 locations throughout the Commonwealth. George takes great pride in pointing out that, although his company has grown rapidly, EasCare has managed to maintain many of the great characteristics of a small, local business. George has served on several boards including the Dorchester Board of Trade and the St. Brendan's Parish Council and Parent's Advisory Board. George is able to trace his family history back to 1691 in Co. Armagh, and their arrival in Boston in 1908. George is a graduate of Don Bosco Technical High School and the University of Massachusetts Boston. He and his wife of 37 years, Mary E. (Mulvey) Gilpin, have proudly lived and raised their two sons in Dorchester.

The Foley Family

Jerry Foley, his sons and his grandsons are carrying on a tradition that began when Jeremiah Foley, Jerry's grandfather, left Co. Kerry and later opened J.J. Foley's Café, a "public house" in the South End in 1909. The family also operates J.J. Foley's Bar & Grill in the Financial District. The Foleys, from left, are **Jeremiah**, **Michael**, **Patrick**, **Jerry**, **Brendan**, and Michael's sons, **Michael**, age 12, and **Flynn**, who was six when this photograph was taken. Jerry and his wife, Marianne, whose family came from Co. Cork, have another son, Reverend Matthew Foley, O.F.M. Conv., a friar-priest who is a religion teacher and campus minister at Archbishop Curley High School in Baltimore. Jerry was raised in Dorchester in St. Matthew's Parish, where he was an altar boy. He has worked in the family business his whole adult life. J.J. Foley's, located on East Berkeley Street, has been a gathering place for neighborhood residents who, particularly during the years of the Big Dig construction, would find themselves next to workers grabbing a late-night meal and MBTA drivers getting off their shift. Countless political gatherings, "times" to benefit one cause or another, and work parties have been held at J.J. Foley's over the years.

Rosalee and David McCullough

Rosalee Barnes and **David McCullough** met as teenagers when she traveled to Pittsburgh where David was born and raised. "How lucky for me," he says. "How very lucky for me." The couple, who married in 1954, has five children and 19 grandchildren. During that time, David, who former President George H.W. Bush called "*the* historian," has written bestselling books about subjects as diverse as the Johnstown Flood, the Brooklyn Bridge, and John Adams. His tenth book, *The Wright Brothers*, is due out in May 2015. David has won two Pulitzer Prizes, two National Book Awards, the Presidential Medal of the Arts, the Presidential Medal of Freedom, and, in 2014, was inducted into the French Legion of Honor. "David McCullough is also, I can assert with unimpeachable authority, a wonderful, an exemplary, father and husband," his son, David McCullough, Jr., wrote in *The Boston Globe*. "And Pop has enjoyed all this, has achieved all this, because he loves and believes in his work." Rosalee's family emigrated from Co. Antrim, and David is quick to point out that his family isn't Irish like Rosalee's, the McCulloughs are Scots-Irish. "Although my family seemed a lot more Irish than Scots, from the way they would tell stories around the table," David says. "They talked a lot, talking about the local history and the family."

Ted English

Bob's Discount Furniture Chairman and CEO **Ted English** started his career in retail as a 15-year-old stock boy at Filene's Basement, took an executive-in-training position when he enrolled in Northeastern University, and later joined T.J.Maxx as a buyer. He spent the next 23 years working in various positions and was named president and CEO in 2000. Ted's paternal grandparents emigrated by boat from Ireland to Boston in the late 19th century. They met here when they landed, then married and settled in South Boston. Ted takes inspiration from his father, Eddie, a hardworking day laborer and World War II veteran who later became an electrician working for the "T" on the night shift. Ted said his father always wanted to take his children to the "Old Country," but it wasn't something they were able to afford. "I made several trips to Ireland as a buyer, scouring the countryside for hand-knit sweaters, and later as CEO, where we operated numerous retail stores called TK Maxx throughout Ireland," Ted says. "I always think of my dad when I'm over there."

The McCourt Family

South Boston–based McCourt Construction built—and rebuilt—every runway and taxiway at Logan International Airport and has served as general contractor for highway, tunnel, bridge, park and utility projects throughout the country. But for **Ryan**, **Trevor**, **Richard**, **Virginia**, and **Matthew McCourt**, Boston is home. Ancestor John McCourt was 13 years old when he left his family's farm in what is now Co. Tyrone, Northern Ireland, and immigrated to Boston in 1860. Here he met and married Sabina Hopkins. While working as a foreman for the Boston Gas Co., John saw a need for skilled private contractors and left his job to open the John McCourt Co. in 1893. When John died in 1915, Sabina ran the company for many years; it was one of the earliest woman-owned construction businesses. The company is now in its fifth generation of family ownership and headed up by Ryan, Matt and Trevor McCourt, while their dad, Richard, who led the company for more than 40 years, is a close adviser. This photograph was taken at the North End Parks, part of the Rose Fitzgerald Kennedy Greenway, which the McCourt company built in 2008. The McCourts have worked hard to give back to their community. They were involved in the building of The Neighborhood House in South Boston and have organized and donated equipment and manpower for "Community Cleanup" days in towns across Massachusetts. The company is active in the McCourt Foundation, which raises money for Alzheimer's Disease and Multiple Sclerosis research.

The Nolan Family

In 1926, Matty Hughes was just 16 when he founded what is now known as Boston Harbor Cruises. His grandchildren and great-grandchildren, the Nolans, now run that company. They are, from left, **Chris**, **Patrick**, **Rick**, **Alison**, and **Mark Nolan**. Matty's family emigrated from Co. Cork at the turn of the last century and his was the first generation born in the United States. The youngest licensed boat captain on Boston Harbor, Matty Hughes started Boston Harbor Cruises as a cruise company taking passengers on sightseeing excursions along the Charles River. Upon his return from serving in the U.S. Navy in World War II, Matty moved his one-ship operation to Boston Harbor. The fleet has grown to 42 vessels in 2014. The business continues to be a family affair. Rick Nolan, a grandson of the founder, met his wife, Heather, who was in the Coast Guard, through work. They have four children. The third and fourth generation of Nolans running the company all live in the Greater Boston area. The company and family are involved in the Boston Harbor Island Association and the USS Constitution Museum. On any given day, you can find a Nolan on Long Wharf, the Boston Harbor Cruise dock in Charlestown or at the helm of a ship.

Margaret Dalton

Margaret Dalton was born in Youghal, Co. Cork, a seaside resort town on the border of Co. Waterford, where her family parish was located. "And with a mother from Galway, I had the best of three counties," Margaret says. It had been her dream to go to America, and so, at age 17, she boarded a plane for Boston. When she arrived some 40 years ago, she started going to Irish dances to meet people and even began singing—something she now does professionally with Erin's Melody. Margaret formed the band in the late 1990s with Colm McDaid and they have recorded many albums and performed at numerous events and fundraisers. Erin's Melody received the Heritage Festival's first Larry Reynolds Spirit Award in 2013. Margaret and her husband Michael McCarron, originally from Co. Donegal, have two children, Owen and Rosemary. "I love to watch from the stage as people forget their troubles for awhile," she says. "I hope to keep the Irish tradition alive through the music and songs for many years to come."

Jay Cashman

Jay Cashman's Irish ancestors were part of the crews that built the Pilgrim Monument in Provincetown at the tip of Cape Cod. The chairman of Cashman Companies now runs one of the country's leading contractors of large-scale projects, such as working on the Big Dig, the Massachusetts Convention and Exhibition Center, construction on Spectacle Island construction, and the Greenbush Commuter Rail line. Jay is photographed at his company's yard in Quincy, not far from where he started in the business by doing marine repair work to seawalls and jetties destroyed in the Blizzard of '78. "It's about working hard for what you believe in," says Jay. "That's always been the family credo: 'Come Monday it's back to the bricks.'" Jay and his wife, Christy, support a number of charities, including Camp Harbor View, PEN/New England, and Massachusetts General Hospital. Jay has worked with genealogists to trace his family tree back generations (his ancestors have ties to Inniscarra, Co. Cork), and he bought Kilkea Castle in Co. Kildare. The renovation work on the castle and its reopening as a hotel is being documented for a television show produced by Christy.

Kevin H. Kelley

Kevin H. Kelley's grandparents emigrated from Co. Donegal to make Boston their home. Kevin has kept that Irish spirit alive through his dedication to community service. Kevin served as the chairman of the Irish American Partnership's annual Boston St. Patrick's Day breakfast, and, in 2012, Kevin received the Solas Award from the Irish International Immigrant Center. The CEO of Ironhorse, Inc., a global specialty property and casualty insurance company, he is credited with expanding the company with a network of new offices around the world. A Boston native, Kevin serves on the boards of several organizations including St. Elizabeth's Medical Center, Big Brothers Big Sisters of Massachusetts Bay, and Cardinal Spellman High School in Brockton, his alma mater. An avid runner, Kevin has run 16 marathons in major cities around the world, including the Boston Marathon in 1996. He is a lifelong Boston Red Sox and Celtics fan, as are his Irish-American wife, Maryellen, and children, an affinity they share with Kevin's ancestors.

Richard F. Gormley

For **Richard F. Gormley** a few things matter above all else: honor, family, faith, and heritage. Shown at the gate of Forest Hills Cemetery in Jamaica Plain, Richie is known to countless people through his family's West Roxbury business, the William J. Gormley Funeral Service. In addition to his Massachusetts funeral director's license, Richie is registered to conduct funerals in Ireland. He served in the U.S. Marine Corps in Vietnam from 1968 to 1970 and received the Cross of Gallantry for his valor. After the war, he traveled to Ireland for the first time and now owns a house on "a nice piece of land" in Ballybrogan, Lecarrow, Co. Roscommon, and travels there several times a year. "Whenever I can," he says. Richie is pictured with a 1937 Packard, one of the classic automobiles he owns, and with Mayor James Michael Curley's top hat that he picked up a few years ago. The hat came in handy when Richie ran for (and won) the election as the unofficial "Mayor of West Roxbury."

Hoteliers

The Irish have a long history in the hospitality industry, and this is particularly true in Boston, where at least seven of the city's leading hoteliers are of Irish descent. They are, from left, **Stephen G. Johnston**, managing director and general manager, the Boston Harbor Hotel; **Ian Pullan**, general manager, InterContinental Boston; **Paul S. Tormey**, general manager and regional vice president, The Fairmont Copley Plaza; **Daniel Donahue**, vice president and managing director, The Lenox Hotel and Boston Common Hotel; **Timothy P. Brett**, area managing director, Pyramid Hotel Group; **James M. Carmody**, vice president and general manager, Seaport Hotel & World Trade Center; and **Thomas P. Walsh**, general manager, Renaissance Boston Waterfront.

Stephen was born in Ireland and worked at a variety of hotels in Ireland and the United Kingdom, but when he assumed the top post at the Boston Harbor Hotel, Stephen was actually returning to his U.S. home. His first trip to Boston was in 1995 when he was managing the U.S. tour of the famous Jurys Irish Cabaret, which played at the Dorothy Quincy Theater in the old John Hancock Building. Little did Stephen know that nine years later he would return to nearly that same spot—just across the street—to open Boston's first Irish-owned hotel, Jurys Boston Hotel (now Loews Boston Hotel) in the former Boston Police headquarters. Since he transferred to Boston from the historic Fairfax at Embassy Row, a Luxury Collection Hotel in Washington D.C., Stephen has become a U.S. citizen.

When Ian arrived in 2013 to run the InterContinental property on Boston HarborWalk at the Fort Point Channel, he came to Boston from The Fairmont Waterfront in Vancouver, British Columbia. A seasoned veteran, Ian got his start as a hall porter at age 16 at FitzPatrick's Shannon Shamrock in Bunratty, Co. Clare. A graduate of the Galway Hotel School in Ireland, Ian has worked in the business for 30 years in jobs that have taken him to seven countries and to 18 properties. Ian was born in Ireland and grew up in Co. Clare. He is now a U.S. citizen. Ian is also an accomplished marathoner; while in Vancouver, he would take guests on guided runs of the city twice a week.

In his role as general manager and regional vice president at The Fairmont Copley Plaza, Paul not only manages the iconic hotel, but is leading the historic property through a $20-million renovation. He also oversees the operations for the Fairmont Battery Wharf in Boston, Fairmont Hamilton Princess and Fairmont Southampton in Bermuda, and the legendary Plaza in New York. With more than 25 years of hotel experience, Paul has held posts throughout North America. He is a graduate of Northeastern University and was raised in Newton, where his grandfather was once chief of police. Paul's great-grandparents came to the United States from Co. Cork. Since returning to Boston seven years ago, Paul has become involved in the community, serving on the advisory board for Boston University's Shaw School of Hospitality and as chairman of the Friends of Copley Square.

Dan grew up in Erie, Pennsylvania, thinking he was destined to be a priest—not uncommon in Irish families—and wound up in the hospitality business. He came to

Boston to help open the Jurys Boston in 2004 and later ran the hotel, which won a number of awards. He previously worked at the Jurys Hotel in Washington, D.C. He has been an active member of the Boston community and serves on the Newbury College board of trustees. His dedication to community shone through after the Boston Marathon bombings, when Dan was credited with helping to reopen his neighborhood. He says his family showed him the value of hard work, particularly grandparents Florence and Jeremiah Donahue, who came from Dublin.

As an area managing director for the Pyramid Hotel Group, Tim oversees four Boston area hotels. This post, which he has held since 2013, came after 10 years with the company. Tim's grandparents were born in Sligo, Ireland, and he holds dual citizenship. A Hingham native and a graduate of University of Massachusetts, Amherst, Tim made a name for himself playing lacrosse. He is a former member of the Irish National Lacrosse Team and represented Ireland in tournaments in four countries. Tim scored the winning goal against Scotland to win the Celtic Cup tournament in Cardiff, Wales, for Ireland's first lacrosse trophy.

Jim, who has been at the Seaport for 10 years, came to running a hotel and one of the city's largest event spaces by way of the kitchen—a familiar place because he grew up in Dorchester as one of eight children. He was 14 when he started cooking full-time at the Howard Johnson in Dorchester (where he would meet his wife, Theresa). He graduated from the Culinary Institute of America and Cornell University's School of Hotel Administration. Growing up, Jim did not know that Irish cuisine is an oxymoron to many. His mother, who was born in Sligo, was a private chef before she married, and his grandmother cooked at Locke-Ober. Jim's father was born in the United States, but lived as a child in Cork before returning to Boston. Jim holds dual passports, as do his wife and four children.

After 27 years working with the Marriott Corporation, Tom moved to running the Renaissance Boston Waterfront at the nexus of South Boston's Innovation District, Seaport District, and the Boston Convention and Exhibition Center at a time of incredible growth. A Salem State graduate, Tom started as a barback at the Burlington Marriott and stayed with the company for nearly three decades, running properties in New York City and Hartford before returning to run the Renaissance in 2013. All of Tom's grandparents hail from Ireland.

Dan Shaughnessy

If you follow Boston sports—even a little bit—then you have read a piece written by **Dan Shaughnessy**. Dan joined *The Boston Globe* in 1981 and has been a sports columnist since 1989. He has been named Massachusetts Sportswriter of the Year 11 times and has been voted one of the country's top 10 sports columnists by the Associated Press Sports Editors 10 times. Dan has written a dozen books, including *The New York Times* best seller *Francona, The Red Sox Years*, which he cowrote with Terry Francona; *The Curse of the Bambino*; and *Senior Year, A Father, A Son, and High School Baseball*. Dan makes regular appearances on The SportsHub 98.5 FM, WHDH-TV's *SportsXtra*, and Comcast SportsNet New England. Born in Groton, Massachusetts, and a graduate of the College of the Holy Cross, the Shaughnessys came from Co. Galway to Cambridge, where Dan's family lived for several generations.

Margaret Coughlin

Margaret Coughlin believes that her Irish heritage is the force that informs her entire life. As the oldest of eight children raised in Westport, Connecticut, she learned that there were key values that ran her "tribe," she says. Her great-grandfather was eight years old when he immigrated to Boston with his older sister. They were separated and he never saw her again. Margaret says that drive has been passed down through the generations. She is the chief marketing and communications officer and senior vice president of Boston Children's Hospital. Margaret says that her Irish background gave her the perseverance to thrive in her career, "in the crazy, competitive world of advertising and marketing." Margaret is a graduate of Skidmore College and received a master's in business administration from Babson College. "When you grow up as an Irish Catholic in a large family, you learn the blessings of living your life in service of others," Margaret says.

Tricia McCorkle

As the director of communications at the TD Garden for nearly 10 years, **Tricia McCorkle** has seen it all. From "Duck Boat" parades celebrating an NBA Championship and a Stanley Cup win, to taking the Ringling Bros. elephants out for a walk, to fan meet-and-greets with rock stars and athletes alike, chances are if you saw it on the news or social media, she was the media maestro behind the scenes. The Boston Strong concert at TD Garden in 2013 was one of her proudest career moments as she was one of the chief organizers of the event. Benefitting The One Fund, the concert raised more than $2.2 million, helping those most affected by the tragic Boston Marathon bombings. Second-generation Irish-American, Tricia's grandmother Winnie was born and raised in Cloonfad, Co. Roscommon, with 13 brothers and sisters and no running water or electricity. Winnie and her husband, Joe, from Castleisland, Co. Kerry, met at an Irish dance in Boston and raised nine children in Jamaica Plain.

Steve Sweeney, Lenny Clarke and Don Gavin

The deans of Boston comedy—**Steve Sweeney**, **Lenny Clarke**, and **Don Gavin**—honed their craft far from the film and television projects and packed houses that they are known for today. They, along with dozens of others, first took the stage at the Ding-Ho, a legendary comedy launching pad that was located in the back room of a Chinese restaurant in Inman Square, Cambridge. "It's really something, if you think about it, we all got our start together as comics…and after 35 or more years we're still friends," Steve (left) says. He is "100-percent Irish"; his mother's family settled in St. Peter's Parish in Dorchester after emigrating from Midleton, in southeastern Co. Cork, and his father's also came from Co. Cork to Charlestown, where Steve was raised. He's not kidding when he tells the stories of his family "vacationing" in Savin Hill during the summers. A veteran of Boston's radio scene, Steve has a dozen or so film credits, including the 2014 Boston–set *The Equalizer*, starring Denzel Washington that topped the box office the weekend it opened. Lenny (center) says the reason that so many Irish Americans found work in the performing arts, particularly writing, acting and comedy, is because "nobody would hire us. I keep a 'No Irish Need Apply' sign in my house to remind me that when other people won't give you a job, you can create your own life," says the comic-actor who has more than four dozen film and television credits. Perhaps best known for his role as "Uncle Teddy" on *Rescue Me*, Denis Leary's award-winning series, Lenny was raised just outside Harvard Square in an area that used to be called "Kerry Corner" for all the families, like the Clarkes, that came from Co. Kerry. Don continues to travel, working and doing stand-up on gigs that take him around the world. Don, a third-generation Irish American, traces his family roots to Co. Galway. He grew up in West Roxbury, which was "98-percent Irish, maybe more." He says he learned to "cherish the three Italian families because you knew that if you went to *their* houses, you'd get great food."

Edward F. Smith and Edward F. Smith Jr.

E.F. Smith & Son Founder and CEO **Edward F. Smith** have built a business on getting people started in the restaurant and pub industry. Shown here in his Quincy, Massachusetts, warehouse with his son, **Edward F. Smith, Jr.**, the company's president, Ed has been in the restaurant equipment auction business since 1973. Ed's father came from Co. Limerick and lived in South Boston before settling in Milton. He says a lot of his family's history was lost when his father died young. The Smith family have been ardent but quiet

supporters of a number of causes over the years. In 1994, Ed Sr., and his wife, Joan, donated a mahogany angel sculpture for the crèche displayed every holiday season on the Dennis Village Green, according to the *Cape Cod Times*. The angel, sculpted by Rhode Island artist Walter Horak, was given in memory of the Smith's daughter, Cynthia, who was killed on December 21, 1988, when a terrorist bomb exploded on Pan Am Flight 103 over Lockerbie, Scotland.

Robert P. Faherty

Since 2008, **Robert P. Faherty** and his all-volunteer organization Cops for Kids with Cancer have raised more than $1.5 million and helped hundreds of Boston-area families struggling to keep their lives together while dealing with a devastating diagnosis. "What these families go through, beyond the illness, puts such a strain on their lives," Bob says. The nonprofit, which runs at least one fundraising event a month, gives $5,000 to each selected family. "We hope to keep people in their homes and able to pay their bills," says Bob, who is a retired Boston Police Department superintendent-in-chief. Bob's family is from Connemara in Co. Galway: His father's side is from the village of Claddagh, and his mother's line is from Maam Cross. The charity began through a friendly golf rivalry between Boston Police Captain John Dow, who died in 2007, and members of Ireland's Garda Síochána, led by Detective Pat Hanlon. The group decided that the money raised from their golf competition would go to a hospital that treated children with cancer, and that idea sparked the creation of the charity.

Jerry York and Jack Parker

Jerry York (left) and **Jack Parker** are two of the most successful coaches in men's collegiate hockey. The regular season games when Jerry's Boston College Eagles would face off against Jack's Boston University Terriers weren't the only times they faced each other. Before these Irish Americans were great coaches, both were elite high school and college players. A Watertown native, Jerry, who began the 2014-2015 season as the winningest coach in NCAA hockey history, was a standout player on the Boston College High School and later Boston College squads. It was not always smooth skating for Jerry. "When I entered BC High and tried out for hockey, I didn't even know how to put all the equipment on properly," Jerry told *The Boston Globe*'s Bob Monahan. "We didn't have Youth Hockey, and the best players always came from towns like Arlington and Melrose." A Somerville native, Jack attended Catholic Memorial High School and Boston University, where he played on three Beanpot Championship teams. "Jack is a winner," Olympic Gold medalist Mike Eruzione told *The Globe* about his former coach. "The kids who play for him are winners. He cares for his kids and they care for him." When he stepped down, Jack had racked up several records during his tenure as head coach, including most wins at one school (897), most Beanpot victories (21), most NCAA tournament appearances (24).

Nancy Kelleher and Evelyn Lauder

Nancy Kelleher (left) was committed to finding a cure for breast cancer years before she was diagnosed in 2008. She is now cancer-free and an even greater champion for finding a cure. Nancy and her husband, Rick Kelleher, were named "Humanitarians of the Year" in 2011 by the Breast Cancer Research Foundation (BCRF). The award was given to the couple by **Evelyn Lauder**, shown in this photograph with Nancy just prior to the award presentation at a gala dinner held at the Museum of Fine Arts, Boston. Evelyn, who died on November 12, 2011, founded the BCRF, which has directed more than $53 million to scientists at New England–based medical institutions to fund

research. "Evelyn taught us all so much about how to support something larger than ourselves," Nancy says, adding that Evelyn would regularly check in on the doctors doing research in Boston. Nancy's great-grandfather Michael James McMahon came to America from Co. Clare in 1870, just shy of his 18th birthday, and settled in Bedford, Massachusetts. He worked as a farmer, and after he and Johanna Mahoney were married, they settled into a small farmhouse where all seven of their children were born. The family eventually owned 50 acres and the last of their children donated part of the land to build St. Michael Church on Concord Road.

Maura Tierney

Maura Tierney's connection with Ireland comes directly from her grandmother. "She was from Leitrim and grew up on a farm. She left for Boston when she was 16, and she only came back once. She met my grandfather in Boston. He was Irish, too," Maura told the *Irish Independent* in early 2011 as she was preparing to open in the play *God of Carnage* at Dublin's Gate Theatre. Maura is the oldest of three children born to Pat, who runs her own real estate company in Hyde Park, and the late Joe Tierney, a Boston City Councilor for 16 years, including five as council president. Joe, who left public life after his unsuccessful bid in 1987 to be mayor, worked as a lawyer until his death on December 13, 2009, at age 68. Best known for her portrayal of Dr. Abby Lockhart on *ER*, Maura has appeared on several TV shows, including *Rescue Me*, *The Good Wife*, and *The Affair*, which premiered in October 2014.

Ted Kelly and Jay Hooley

Ted Kelly (right) shares a laugh with **Jay Hooley** at the 2011 Inner-City Scholarship Fund dinner to raise money for The Catholic Schools Foundation, a charity both men actively support. Born in Ireland, Ted graduated from Queen's College in Belfast, Northern Ireland, and earned a doctorate in mathematics at Massachusetts Institute of Technology. Ted stepped down as chairman of Liberty Mutual Group in 2013. He joined the company in 1993 as president, became chief executive five years later, and added the title of chairman in 2000. Ted retired as CEO in 2011, but he remains active in supporting the city's cultural and civic organizations. He sits on several boards, including the American Ireland Fund, and is chairman of the Boston Symphony Orchestra Board of Trustees. Jay is chairman, president, and CEO of State Street Corporation, a Boston–based financial services company serving a broad range of institutional clients with operations in 29 countries, including a major presence in Ireland. On Jay's first day as State Street's CEO in March 2010, he was in Dublin to open the company's new building in the heart of the city. Jay, whose grandparents emigrated from Ireland to the United States, has kept close to his largely Co. Cork–based Irish roots, including the picturesque port of Kinsale. A native of Boston and graduate of Boston College, he's actively engaged in a wide range of charitable and civic causes, including the Catholic Schools Foundation's Inner-City Scholarship Fund, and the American Ireland Fund, where he serves on both the national board of directors and the Boston regional advisory board. Jay also serves on the boards of the Boys & Girls Clubs of Boston, Massachusetts General Hospital, and the Massachusetts Competitive Partnership.

Tom Brady

Tom Brady is proud of his Irish roots and spoke about them at length to reporters when the New England Patriots played the Tampa Bay Buccaneers at Wembley Stadium in 2009. "My father is 100-percent Irish. We took a trip over there together and visited some of the places where my family came from," Tom said. "That was a great experience for me, and, obviously, I am very proud of my Irish roots." The three-time Super Bowl champion has said his work ethic comes from his family. The quarterback's father has spoken of that history with *Irish America*. He told the bimonthly glossy magazine that his great-grandfather, who was from Co. Cavan, and great-grandmother, who came from Co. Cork, immigrated to the United States during the famine years. As a professional athlete with a remarkable career, Tom has used his status to help charitable causes, chiefly Best Buddies, a nonprofit founded by Anthony K. Shriver that works to create opportunities for people with intellectual and developmental disabilities. This photograph was taken at Harvard Stadium at the flag football game that Tom hosts each year to benefit Best Buddies.

The Burke Family

The Burkes say they learned the value of service to others from their father, John F. Burke, who owned and operated a pharmacy for 53 years at the corner of D and West Sixth streets in South Boston's "lower end." He closed his pharmacy during World War II, enlisted, and served for three years in a hospital division in England. John's sons shown here are, from left, Dr. **Dennis W. Burke**, an orthopedic surgeon at Massachusetts General Hospital; Boston Fire Department District Chief **Paul T. Burke**, who was awarded the Commissioner's Citation for his action during the 2013 Boston Marathon bombing; and **John F. Burke**, senior vice president at Staples Corporation and president of the Staples Foundation Board. (Not shown in this photograph are Jacquelyn Burke Graziano, a registered pharmacist like her father, and Michael J. Burke, who retired after 38 years as a member of Local 17 Sheet Metal Workers Union.) John and his wife, Ellie, raised their five children in South Boston, and all attended St. Peter School. John's parents, Bridget and Michael, were from the Aran Islands and settled in Boston. Michael was a cooper and Bridget worked as a domestic. Ellie's parents emigrated from Lithuania and settled in Kingston, Pennsylvania, where her father worked as a coal miner. She moved to Boston when she was 17 years old.

John Henning and Jack Hynes

Veteran television broadcaster **Jack Hynes** had come to Amrheins restaurant in South Boston after the funeral to toast his late friend **John Henning**, a longtime radio and television reporter and commentator, who died on July 7, 2010. (Jack is holding a photograph of John with Playboy Bunnies at the former Playboy Club, which was located at what is now the Four Seasons Hotel.) Jack was born in Boston, the oldest of five children, and raised in St. Gregory's Parish. According to historian Thomas H. O'Connor's account, Jack was home from his freshman year at Notre Dame for his father's January 2, 1950, inauguration as mayor. John B. Hynes would serve as mayor until 1960 and oversee an unprecedented period of growth. Jack is the grandson of Bernard Hynes of Abbey Street, Loughrea, Co. Galway, who arrived in Boston in June 1888. Jack is best known for his calm, steady presence at the television news desk, first at WCVB for 26 years and then, after a brief stint at WBZ, at WLVI (Channel 56) anchoring "The 10 O'Clock News." John Henning, a member of the Broadcasting Hall of Fame, was born in New York City and was a news reporter and anchor at the three major network affiliates for 25 years. Most viewers got to know him for covering thousands of stories—including the political beat—for WBZ-TV (Channel 4).

Jim Cotter

When it came time to recognize the accomplishments of Boston College High School's former football coach **Jim Cotter**, hundreds of people celebrated at their alma mater, including former players (from left) **Michael Merbonne**, **Mike Brennan**, and **Brendan Sullivan**. They came to celebrate the release of Jim's autobiography, *The Coach Jim Cotter Story, A True Man for Others*, written with Paul Kenney. Jim, who retired from coaching in 2004, died on July 20, 2010, from complications of ALS, a disease he battled for four years. Named for his grandfather, Jim was raised by his parents, Dixie and Leslie "Les" Cotter, a longshoreman and a stevedore, with his two brothers in St. William's Parish in Savin Hill. He had three children with his first wife, Ann Grace, who died in 1983. The next year, he married Agnes Donahue, also from Dorchester. Jim played football at Boston College High School and at Boston College. He originally signed on as an assistant coach in 1960 and became head coach four seasons later. In his 41 years on the sidelines, the Eagles had 35 winning seasons, chalking up 232 wins.

Bob Davis

Bob Davis founded Lycos in 1995 and it became the most visited Internet site in the world. He advised President Bill Clinton on issues relating to Internet commerce and regulation, and he has addressed the U.S. Congress, the United Nations, the National Press Corps, and the U.S. Council of Foreign Relations. But Bob always keeps his Dorchester roots front of mind; the Boston neighborhood is marked on the world map on a ceiling in his home. Three of Bob's grandparents emigrated from Ireland, including a grandfather who left Co. Galway for America. By the time Bob was 20 years old, both of his parents were dead so his "life has been all bootstrapped," he says. Bob paid for his classes at Northeastern by working 40 hours a week at a supermarket while attending school. After receiving his Northeastern degree, he went on to earn an MBA from Babson College. Among the many charities that he supports are Bridge Over Troubled Waters and Boston Children's Hospital.

John King

As CNN's chief national correspondent and anchor of the weekly show *Inside Politics*, **John King** has traveled the world to cover the biggest stories of our time. Yet, at heart, he remains "OFD." John says, "Originally From Dorchester is a source of great pride because, like so many, I had parents who had almost nothing and yet somehow gave us everything." John's father was from an Irish-Catholic corner of Lower Mills, and his mother's family (a Scottish dad and an Irish mother) lived on *King Street*. "The joke is that my dad needed to live there for his ego and went door-to-door 'til he found a girl," John says. He is the third of seven children who were raised on the top floor of that three-decker on King Street. John went to the parish elementary school and graduated from Boston Latin before heading off to the University of Rhode Island. But all roads lead back to where he grew up, a place that he described to a *Boston Globe* reporter as "beautiful Dorchester, Massachusetts, God's country. St. Mark's Parish, between Ashmont and Fields Corner."

Joey McIntyre

Actor and singer **Joey McIntyre** does a lot of charity work, but his support of the Massachusetts Eye and Ear is personal. As parents of a child with severe hearing loss, Joey and his wife, Barrett, are supporters of its Curing Kids Fund and its annual gala, where this photograph was taken in 2013. Joey grew up in Jamaica Plain and attended Catholic Memorial High School. He was just 13 when he joined the New Kids on the Block, the Boston–based pop phenoms who have sold more than 80 million records. In May 2014, the band played Dublin, which prompted Joey to do some research into his Irish roots, he told reporters. "My great-grandfather was from Limerick, and he ended up in Boston," he says. Joey's father, Tom, named the youngest of his nine children after Joe Mulrey, founder of the South Boston restaurant Amrheins. Joey, who performed on Broadway in *Wicked*, is featured in *The McCarthys*, a new CBS television series about an Irish-Catholic family in Boston that premiered in fall 2014.

Donnie, Alma, Paul, and Mark Wahlberg

This time the red carpet was rolled out and the media were gathered to celebrate chef **Paul Wahlberg**'s prowess in the kitchen. Building on the success of his Hingham restaurant Alma Nove—named for his mother, **Alma Wahlberg**, with a nod to her nine children—Paul and his brothers **Donnie** and **Mark** opened Wahlburgers, just across the road in the Shipyard. "He's not a fake chef, he's the real deal," Donnie told reporters at the 2013 grand opening. "It really started with Paul. [He] wanted to open a great burger joint in Hingham, and once we all got involved, it kind of took a life of its own." The Wahlbergs have opened more "burger joints" in other cities, and the eatery spawned *Wahlburgers*, a reality television show that follows the three brothers as they expand Paul's restaurant empire. The 30-minute show, which debuted in 2014 on the A&E cable channel, gave the world a new Wahlberg star, Alma. While the Wahlbergs grew up in Dorchester, the Wahlberg family tree includes ancestors by the names of Bradley, Doherty, Dunn, and Donnelly (Alma's maiden name) from Co. Galway and other parts of Ireland who came via Canada. Donnie, who married TV personality Jenny McCarthy in 2014, plays an Irish New York Police detective on *Blue Bloods*, and also produced *Boston's Finest*, a documentary television show that followed members of the Boston Police Department. Mark, who was nominated for an Academy Award for *The Departed*, played "Irish" Micky Ward in *The Fighter*, a film about the Lowell-bred boxing champ, among other roles.

Kay Hanley

Kay Hanley has performed all over the world before huge crowds, appeared in movies, provided the singing voice for cartoons, and performed the national anthem for the New England Patriots. But she remains at heart an Irish-Catholic girl from Dorchester. "It's who I am to my marrow," she says. Her fondest memories from childhood include "[listening to] *The Irish Hour*, an all-day radio program, of course, every Saturday in my Dad's car, running errands along Dot Ave and Gallivan Boulevard." She is best known as the singer for the alternative band Letters to Cleo and for her work with

"Hot Stove Cool Music," the annual concerts to benefit The Foundation To Be Named Later, which brings her back to Boston regularly. Kay says her work is informed by those indelible impressions of the music from her youth when she "committed to memory incredible songs like *Four Green Fields*, *A Nation Once Again*, and *Black Velvet Band*." It's always with her, she said. "How could music be so painful, funny, angry, joyful, deeply poetic, utilitarian all at the same time?" Kay asks. "Those songs, that music, made so much inherent sense to me—to us—they still do."

Nun Day at Fenway Park, 1968

Some 50 years ago, Fenway Park's annual Nun Day drew hundreds of sisters from various religious orders to the storied park to watch a Red Sox game. In any given year, Boston's archbishop, Cardinal **Richard J. Cushing**, an avid fan, was likely to join the nuns in cheering on the home team. The tradition faded out over the ensuing years but was revived in 2013. At left is Bill Brett's sister, **Peg McCobb**, then Sister Sean Patrice of the Sisters of St. Joseph. Peg, the daughter of immigrants from Co. Sligo, left the order and married Bill McCobb, and they raised five children. Bill died in 1998 at age 66. This photograph of the cardinal, wearing his straw hat and black suit, was taken at a very busy time for the South Boston native who led the archdiocese from 1944 to 1970. In 1968, he dedicated what is now Good Samaritan Hospital in Brockton and kept busy raising funds for a $50-million capital campaign. A close friend of the Kennedy family, the cardinal officiated at the marriage of John F. Kennedy and Jacqueline Bouvier in 1953, and celebrated the president's funeral Mass in Washington, D.C. Born in 1895, he was the third of Patrick and Mary Cushing's five children. Patrick emigrated from Glanworth, Co. Cork, while Mary came from Touraneena, Co. Waterford. Richard graduated from Boston College High School and Boston College and was ordained in 1921. He died at age 75 on November 4, 1970.

Bill McQuillan and Peter Meade

The November 2, 2012, "topping off" ceremony for the Residence Inn Marriott Back Bay/Fenway on Brookline Avenue was a big day for developer **Bill McQuillan** (left) of Boylston Properties and a part of the city—near Fenway Park, the Longwood Medical area, and several colleges—which had a dearth of hotel space. In this portrait, Boston Redevelopment Authority Director **Peter Meade** joins Bill in signing the last steel beam to be put atop the eight-story, 175-suite hotel. Bill's Irish-American family, including paternal grandparents Patrick and Rose McQuillan, spent his early years in a three-family house on Topliff Street in Dorchester. Bill started working as a real estate developer in 1978, straight out of Babson College. His projects include the Longwood Galleria at Boston Children's Hospital and the Wellesley headquarters for Harvard Pilgrim Health Care in 2000. With partner Steve Samuels, Bill pushed the rebirth of the Fenway neighborhood with the 2004

start of Trilogy, a $200-million 570-unit apartment building in the heart of that area. He was the board president of the Huntington Theatre Company from 2002 to 2009 and was a trustee and chair of the Building Committee at Babson College. When he was young, Peter's Dorchester house—in St. Ann's Parish—was often a stopping place for musicians, particularly those traveling from his mother's ancestral hometowns of Doolin and Miltown Malbay in Co. Clare. Peter's father, whose family came from Co. Sligo, was involved in a host of Irish cultural and civic organizations. He served as the Boston Redevelopment Authority director from 2011 to 2014 and previously held executive posts at Blue Cross Blue Shield of Massachusetts and The New England Council. He was also the founding chairman of the Rose Fitzgerald Kennedy Conservancy Greenway and former chair of the Emerson College Board of Trustees.

St. Patrick's Day, 1968

Shortly after Senator **Robert F. Kennedy's** March 16, 1968, announcement that he was seeking the presidency, the call came for a young leader, a nonpolitician, to march with the candidate and his brother Senator **Edward M. Kennedy** in Boston's St. Patrick's Day Parade. **James T. Brett** (center), a senior at South Boston High School at the time, was chosen to march the route along Broadway as people crowded to see the Kennedys. This photograph, taken on Dorchester Street, stirs great memories for Jim. "It is remarkable looking back on it. I remember things now, but it was a whirlwind that day. I do remember how people just wanted to be near Bobby Kennedy." (Also in the photograph, back left, is **James B. King**, who has had a decades-long career working in government and at Boston area universities.) The younger brother of Bill Brett, Jim is president and CEO of The New England Council and previously served for more than 15 years as a state representative. Jim attended American University and received master's degrees from Suffolk University and Harvard's Kennedy School of Government. He served as chairman of the President's Committee for People with Intellectual Disabilities, chairman of the Governor's Commission on Intellectual Disability, and president of the board of the Massachusetts Association for Mental Health. Jim is also a member of the board of the John F. Kennedy Library Foundation. "I instinctively understood," says Jim, whose family hails from Co. Sligo, "that in my own small way I was part of history, walking in the company of two brothers, both U.S. Senators, one from New York and one from Massachusetts, who made such a profound impact on our lives."

Margot and Bill Connell

Microsoft cofounder **Bill Gates** stops for a moment at a Boston event to talk with Boston philanthropists **Margot** and **Bill Connell**. The son of Irish immigrants, Bill's first job was selling newspapers in Lynn's McDonough Square, and he went on to found the Boston-based Connell Limited Partnership, a group of manufacturing companies in the auto, energy, mining, construction, and agricultural sectors. Bill, who died on August 22, 2001, at age 63, and his wife supported an array of civic organizations, particularly those that helped shape the Connell family. Often done quietly, the Connells gave several donations to area schools, including $1 million to his alma mater St. Mary's of Lynn, a gift that is said to have kept the high school afloat. They also donated $1 million to establish a scholarship fund at Boston College, where Bill graduated in 1959, for St. Mary's graduates and residents of West Lynn. And, just about a month before Bill died, the Connells donated $10 million to the Boston College School of Nursing, which now bears his name. Following her husband's death, Margot, who taught science and math in elementary schools in California and New York after graduating from Michigan State University, continues the family philanthropy. In 2013, the Connells donated $10 million to the Harvard Business School, from which Bill received his MBA, to support curriculum innovation.

Aogán Ó Fearghaíl and Bernie O'Reilly

Aogán Ó Fearghaíl (left), the newly-minted president of the Gaelic Athletic Association (GAA), made the trip from Ireland to Canton, Massachusetts, for the finals of the North American Gaelic Games over Labor Day weekend in 2014. Aogán came to see the 2,500 players in competition at the Irish Cultural Centre's fields, but he had another purpose. He was on hand to congratulate **Bernie O'Reilly**, who was retiring after 56 years of working with the GAA's Boston branch. The two have a bond beyond football—they are both from Co. Cavan. Aogán is the first Cavan president in the 130-year history of the GAA. Bernie, owner of O'Reilly's Auto Body in Watertown, remembers the day he arrived from Ireland—February 20, 1958—because there was snow on the ground. "It was cold and dark," Bernie says. He landed a job working with Smith and Reilly Contractors and started playing Gaelic football "straight away." Over the years, Bernie has held "every position" with the Boston GAA, including two years as the regional branch president. (A brother Sean O'Reilly would also hold the presidency for two years in the Philadelphia area.) Football was a wonderful outlet, Bernie says, as he was building his business and starting a family. He was a half forward for the Boston-based Cork team and played 15 years with the senior squad, winning three senior championship medals and two junior championship medals. Asked about his prowess on the pitch, Bernie says without a hint of a boast: "When a Cavan man is captain of a Cork team, he's got to be good."

John A. Kelley

John A. Kelley's favorite song was *Young at Heart*, which was also an apt description of the Boston Marathon legend. Johnny is shown here at a statue at the foot of the route's famed Heartbreak Hill, dedicated to him in 1993. The oldest of 10 children in an Irish-American family, Johnny was 12 when his father first took him to watch the Boston Marathon, and he was hooked on running thereafter. He won the Boston Marathon twice, and when the next American winner of the race, Johnny J. Kelley (no relation)

won, Johnny A. Kelley became known as "Kelley the Elder." When the latter died on October 4, 2004, at age 97, Frank Litsky wrote in *The New York Times* that Johnny "was a Boston sports hero in the mold of Ted Williams, Bill Russell, Larry Bird, and Bobby Orr, but of that illustrious group the only one homegrown and the only amateur. He ran perhaps 1,500 races, including 112 marathons, and won 22 diamond rings, 118 watches, one refrigerator, and no money."

James F. and Barbara Cleary

Depression-era babies, born in Malden and Dorchester to modest means, **Barbara (Coliton)** and **James F. Cleary** worked hard to achieve their place as one of Boston's Irish-American power couples. The Cleary family is from Co. Cork and immigrated to Dorchester in the late 19th century. Barbara's family came from the counties of Waterford and Roscommon. She traded a career in the fashion industry to become one of Boston's most cherished hostesses. After graduating from Boston Latin School, Jim enlisted in the U.S. Navy on his seventeenth birthday, serving in the Pacific for two years. He attended Boston College on the GI Bill and began a commitment to Boston College that would last the rest of his life. He was president of Blyth, Eastman Dillon & Co. in New York, and, later, a managing director of Paine Webber, and advisory director of UBS in Boston. Jim served as a Boston College trustee from 1972 to 1996 and as a trustee associate from 1997 to 2012. Jim, who was married to Barbara for 50 years, died on February 26, 2012 at age 89. Barbara and Jim were longtime supporters of the American Ireland Fund and the Boston Symphony Orchestra. In 1993, they founded Boston College's "Pops on the Heights" gala, which has raised more than $22 million to fund more than 800 scholarships. It is the university's largest annual fundraiser.

Joseph F. Timilty, John F. Collins, and Joe Moakley

This photograph is the earliest photograph in this book. It was a late night for three leading Boston politicians in 1967 when Bill Brett captured this scene while on assignment downtown. **Joseph F. Timilty** (left) was in his first year on the City Council, **John F. Collins** (center) was in the final days of his eight-year tenure as Boston's 50th mayor, and **Joe Moakley** was then serving as state Senator, representing South Boston. John worked up to his last hours in office, overseeing projects begun while he was mayor, including the construction of the new City Hall. The Collins family traces its lineage from Northern Ireland and from Ireland via New Brunswick, Canada. "John Collins was a hands-on mayor," Joe Timilty says. "Things were different back then. You could fight politically with someone during the day, and the next day you were working right beside them." The Timiltys are from Co. Roscommon and have been in Boston for "at least six generations," Joe says. His family has also given a century of public service to Boston and beyond. Joe's grandfather was a state Senator, and the James P. Timilty Middle School in Roxbury was named in his honor in 1937. Joe Timilty later served as state Senator and ran three unsuccessful campaigns to be mayor of Boston—1971, 1975, and 1979. Joe and his wife, Elaine, raised their seven children in St. Gregory's Parish in Dorchester.

Séamus Connolly

One of the world's most respected master Irish musicians, **Séamus Connolly** is Boston College's Sullivan artist-in-residence, won the Irish National Fiddle Competition an unprecedented 10 times and has performed on more than two dozen recordings. A native of Killaloe, Co. Clare, Séamus says he grew up in a house filled with music; his parents and two brothers were musicians. (His brother Martin, a button accordionist, also won the Irish National championship several times.) Séamus was 12 years old when he began playing the fiddle, and it seems like he has not slowed down since. Nor have the accolades. In 2002, Séamus was inducted into the "Hall of Fame" of Comhaltas Ceoltóirí Éireann. In 1972, Séamus came to the United States as a member of the first CCE tour, and he immigrated to America in 1976, settling in the Boston area. At the request of Larry Reynolds, president of the local branch of CCE, Séamus agreed to teach Irish fiddling to American-born students, and he's been teaching and entertaining ever since.

Tom Flatley

This is a rare photograph of **Tom Flatley** because the self-made, hard-charging businessman wasn't one to don a tuxedo just for show. A philanthropist, Tom quietly gave away millions to a variety of causes, including Catholic Charities, Boston College, St. Anselm College, Africa relief and Irish causes, and the New England Shelter for Homeless Veterans, and he didn't do it for the recognition. He was always working—on behalf of his company or for a cause. The commercial real estate company that bore his name had an estimated value of $1.3 billion when he died in 2008 at age 76. Tom kept a bit of his Irish brogue from his youth and all of the work ethic he learned on his family's 25-acre farm in Co. Mayo where he was born and raised. A daily communicant, Tom cherished his adopted country and, although private, was fiercely proud of his family—his wife, Charlotte, their five children and 18 grandchildren. The $1 million Irish Famine Memorial in downtown Boston, unveiled in 1998 to commemorate the 150th anniversary of the depths of *An Gorta Mór* (The Great Hunger), is one of the lasting legacies of Tom's hard work and love of Boston.

The Corcoran Family

Corcoran Jennison Companies Chairman **Joseph E. Corcoran** used his success as one of the region's largest real estate developers and managers to help those for whom housing isn't a certainty. Under Joe's leadership, the Dorchester-based company has developed more than $2.5 billion worth of projects and is credited with pioneering the concept of mixed-income housing. Joe was born one of eight children to John and Mary (Merrigan) Corcoran, who emigrated from Roscommon and raised their family in the Uphams Corner neighborhood of Dorchester. Joe is shown here with daughters **Suzanne Corcoran Early** (left) and **Kathryn Dean**, two of seven children with wife, Rosemarie, who died in April 2014. Joe, a graduate of Boston College High School and Boston College, started in the real estate business with his brothers. They were among the business leaders who supported the American Ireland Fund at its start in the 1970s. Joe also founded the American City Coalition, a nonprofit organization that plans and implements the revitalization of urban neighborhoods.

The O'Neil Sisters

Their photographs appeared in *Life* and *Newsweek* magazines and newspapers around the world. The 10 O'Neil sisters of Jamaica Plain were known in the 1940s and 1950s for their appearances in Boston's annual Easter parade walking side-by-side in identical outfits hand-sewn by their mother, Julia. Eight of the O'Neil sisters gathered at Doyle's in Jamaica Plain to celebrate the birthday of **Jane Deery** (seated at far right) in August 2007. From left, **Julie O'Neil** (behind bench), **Maureen Cloonan**, **Diane Nessar**, **Danielle McGreal**, **Evelyn Kiley**, **Frances Cummings**, and **Ginny O'Neil**. Jane died on September 26, 2012, in Boston. **Mary June Hanrahan** was not at the celebration and the second-oldest sister, **Barbara Wampole**, died in 2000. (The sisters had two brothers, who bookended the 10 girls: Lawrence, the oldest, died in 1990, and Daniel Jr., died in 2010.) Their father, Daniel, is said to have loved watching his daughters strolling on Commonwealth Avenue Mall in their holiday finest alongside the Boston Brahmins. The O'Neil family came from Ireland to Nova Scotia before heading to Boston. The 10 sisters also sang and performed and made appearances on *The Ed Sullivan Show*, the *Today* show, and with Steve Allen, and continued to make appearances until their father died in the late 1950s.

Barbara Lynch

Barbara Lynch is one the leaders of Boston's culinary world, but this working-class Irish chef and restaurateur did not always have an easy path. "I grew up seven minutes from here," Barbara told the crowd at a TEDx lecture at the University of Massachusetts Boston. "We lived in the Mary Ellen McCormack Housing Project. I'm the youngest of seven, raised by a single mom." Barbara's father died a month before she was born. Today, Barbara oversees a $25-million restaurant group that includes No. 9 Park, B&G Oysters, and Menton. A James Beard Award winner, Barbara was an early supporter of iFest, a celebration of Irish culture that had its inaugural run in South Boston in 2014. In preparation for iFest, Barbara took her first trip to Ireland on a culinary tour of Cork and Killarney. In 2012, she launched the Barbara Lynch Foundation; its mission is "to empower urban youth in at-risk Boston communities with essential life skills."

Joe O'Donnell

One of the city's leading entrepreneurs, **Joe O'Donnell** has also used his skills to raised hundreds of millions of dollars for charity. The Joey Fund, which Joe and his wife, Kathy, founded in honor of their son Joey, who died at age 12 of cystic fibrosis, became the primary focus of their philanthropic efforts. Joe credits his upbringing with giving him the foundation to achieve business success. "I grew up in a solidly lower-middle-class, blue-collar area in Everett, Massachusetts," Joe told an interviewer from the Harvard Business School. "My father was a policeman. My mother was a housewife and had been valedictorian of her class. She was first-generation Italian, and my father was first-generation Irish." The founder of Boston Concessions, which has since merged with Centerplate, Joe is a graduate of Harvard College and the Harvard Business School. He started his first concession business while still in high school, renting out tuxedos for the prom at Malden Catholic. Joe endowed Harvard's baseball program, and, in 1997, the university named a field in honor of the former baseball and football standout.

John T. O'Connor

John T. O'Connor accomplished much in his lifetime. He was a longtime environmental activist, an author, a developer, leader of the National Toxics Campaign, chairman of Gravestar, Inc., founder of Greenworks, and a onetime candidate for Congress. John died suddenly in late 2001 after suffering an apparent heart attack while playing basketball in Cambridge. He was 46. "John was a great man, and the world is a better place because of his compassion, great love and unyielding drive to help other people," his wife, Carolyn Mugar, told *The Boston Globe* for his obituary. John was the cofounder of the committee that created the Irish Famine Memorial on Cambridge Common, which was dedicated by Irish President Mary T. Robinson in 1997. John's great-grandfather John came to the United States in 1847 as a teenager with his brother Richard. The admitting documents list only "Ireland" as country of origin—no village or county was recorded. They first settled in Malden and got jobs in agriculture as field hands. John and Richard learned of better jobs in Connecticut so they walked all the way to Waterbury. That determination was passed down through generations to John, who was one of six children born to Kay and George O'Connor of Stratford, Connecticut.

Mayor Kevin H. White

On Tuesday, November 7, 1967, Massachusetts Secretary of State **Kevin H. White** won the Boston mayoral election in a close race against School Committee member Louise Day Hicks. This photograph was taken as Kevin and his wife, **Kathryn**, took the stage for a victory speech that marked the beginning of the first of his four terms. Kevin, who died on January 27, 2012, was the tenth mayor of Boston to claim Irish heritage, but it was the support of other ethnic groups that helped get him to the mayor's office.

One of Kevin's biggest supporters can be seen at left, state Senator **Mario Umana**, a powerful figure in East Boston, who, after two dozen years in the State House, wrapped up his career as a municipal court judge. The son and grandson of Boston City Council presidents, Kevin grew up in Jamaica Plain and West Roxbury. Kathryn also came from a political family. She was one of the seven daughters of William J. "Mother" Galvin, a former Boston City Council president from Charlestown.

The funeral of Speaker John W. McCormack

From his neighbors to the vice president of the United States at the time, thousands came to St. Monica Church in South Boston to pay their respects to the former U.S. Speaker of the House **John W. McCormack**, who died on November 22, 1980, at age 88. Born in South Boston, John rose from his position as a trial lawyer to the Massachusetts State House, where he served in the U.S. Congress for 34 years, including nine years as Speaker. An eighth-grade dropout, John studied law at night and was admitted to the Massachusetts Bar at age 21. His grandparents on both sides of his family left Ireland during the great wave of immigration of the 1840s. When John and his beloved wife, Harriet, who died in 1971, were married in 1920, she gave up a promising career with the Metropolitan Opera Company of New York. Shown in this photograph are the Speaker's nephew **Edward J. McCormack**, Jr., former Massachusetts Attorney General, and his wife, **Emily**, who are being escorted by **John O'Connor** (center) of the John J. O'Connor & Son Funeral Home in Dorchester. To the right are then Vice President **George H.W. Bush**, and former House Speaker **Thomas P. "Tip" O'Neill**, Jr. and U.S. Speaker **Carl Albert** of Oklahoma.

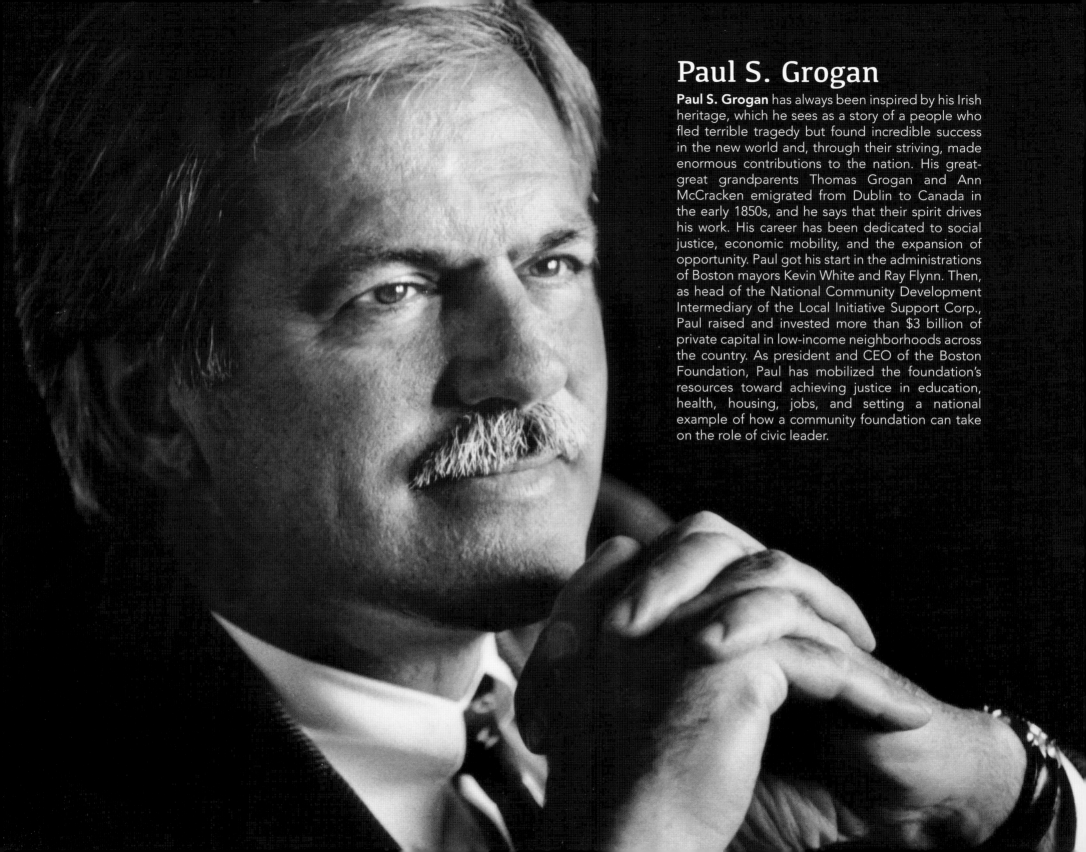

Paul S. Grogan

Paul S. Grogan has always been inspired by his Irish heritage, which he sees as a story of a people who fled terrible tragedy but found incredible success in the new world and, through their striving, made enormous contributions to the nation. His great-great grandparents Thomas Grogan and Ann McCracken emigrated from Dublin to Canada in the early 1850s, and he says that their spirit drives his work. His career has been dedicated to social justice, economic mobility, and the expansion of opportunity. Paul got his start in the administrations of Boston mayors Kevin White and Ray Flynn. Then, as head of the National Community Development Intermediary of the Local Initiative Support Corp., Paul raised and invested more than $3 billion of private capital in low-income neighborhoods across the country. As president and CEO of the Boston Foundation, Paul has mobilized the foundation's resources toward achieving justice in education, health, housing, jobs, and setting a national example of how a community foundation can take on the role of civic leader.

David M. Bartley, Thomas W. McGee, Timothy J. Taylor

This celebratory moment marked the end of a six-year political battle over reducing the size of the Massachusetts House when a joint constitutional convention voted on the measure on June 7, 1973. Although House Speaker **David M. Bartley** (left) looks happy as he greets state Representative **Thomas W. McGee**, then House Majority leader, the two were not proponents of making the House smaller. These two Irish-American politicians were part of an unlikely coalition whose members thought reducing the Legislature from 240 members to 160 would give favor to the wealthy suburbs closer to Boston. The measure was approved by voters and implemented in 1979. Dave, who is from Holyoke, was House Speaker from 1969 to 1975 and also served as Secretary of Administration and Finance in the King Administration. Tom, who represented Lynn, succeeded Dave as House Speaker and held the position until 1984. He died on December 21, 2012, at age 88. **Timothy J. Taylor** (right), was a reporter for the *Boston Herald Traveler* who served as press secretary for three House Speakers. Tim died on December 7, 2011, at age 72.

Will McDonough

Will McDonough was an education major at Northeastern University when he was sent on his first cooperative education assignment as a student teacher. Will didn't get along with the school administration, so Northeastern decided to "punish" him by making his next work assignment as a copy boy on the overnight desk at *The Boston Globe*'s sports department. For Will, an accomplished student-athlete, it was the greatest assignment of his life. His columns became a must-read for a sports-obsessed city and he would work at *The Globe*—except for a brief hiatus—until his death in 2003. Will was the youngest of nine children born to Martin and Katherine McDonough, who both came to America from Galway in the early 20th century. In 1974, he took the unprecedented action of fighting for and winning custody of his three children: Sean, a broadcaster for ESPN; Erin, chief communication officer at Brigham and Women's Hospital; and Terence, vice president of Player Personnel for the Arizona Cardinals. Will married Denise in 1978, and they had two more children, Ryan, general manager for the Phoenix Suns, and Cara, director of global e-commerce for Under Armour.

Sister Mary Black

Elnora Miles greets her former teacher **Sister Mary** (right) at a 2010 celebration marking her 50th anniversary of dedicated service to Cathedral High School in the South End. Sister Mary taught math and physics for 25 years and was involved in just about every department at the high school. She "retired" in 2012 and remains involved with Cathedral, including working on two development events in fall 2014. "I won't ever say I'm truly retired," she says. Sister Mary (the former Eugene Marie) also works tirelessly for the Office of Mission Advancement for the Sisters of St. Joseph. Sister Mary's family came to America in the mid-19th century from Co. Cavan, stopping first in South Boston before settling in Medway, where the eighth generation of her family lives. "When I left 65 years ago, that was farm country," she says. All roads seem to lead her back to Cathedral. "It is obvious from all the people who came what an impact she had on the lives of so many of her former students," Cardinal Seán P. O'Malley wrote on his blog.

Carolyn Bessette Kennedy and John F. Kennedy, Jr.

John F. Kennedy, Jr. and his wife, **Carolyn Bessette Kennedy**, enjoy the arrival of family and friends at the John F. Kennedy Presidential Library and Museum for the May Dinner, the annual event held to celebrate the life and legacy of his father and to bestow the Profile in Courage Award. Just two months after this photograph was taken, the couple died on July 16, 1999, when the small plane John was piloting crashed into the Atlantic Ocean just off the coast of Martha's Vineyard. Carolyn's sister Lauren, who was traveling with them, also died. The only sibling of Caroline Kennedy, John ran *George*, the monthly, political lifestyle magazine that he cofounded in 1995. John, who is said to have not used either his middle initial or Jr. on his business cards, attended Brown University and studied law at New York University. Very much like his sister, John supported a number of charities and worked on behalf of those in need. Born and educated in New York, Carolyn graduated from Boston University.

Caroline Kennedy

Scion of Boston's most prominent Irish family, U.S. Ambassador **Caroline Kennedy**, keeps the Kennedy history alive through her work with the John F. Kennedy Presidential Library and Museum on Dorchester's Columbia Point, and as honorary president of the JFK Library Foundation. Caroline was nominated by President Barack Obama and later sworn in as the U.S. ambassador to Japan by Secretary of State John Kerry on November 12, 2013. The daughter of President John F. Kennedy and Jacqueline Kennedy Onassis, Caroline graduated from Harvard and received a law degree from Columbia University. In addition to her work with the Library, much of Caroline's professional life has been dedicated to social issues and politics, including her address at the 2008 Democratic National Convention. Caroline has traveled to the family homestead in Dunganstown, Co. Wexford, including attending the June 2013 ceremony to commemorate the 50th anniversary of President Kennedy's trip to Ireland as the first—and only, as the Irish press point out—Irish-Catholic U.S. president.

Joseph P. Kennedy II and III

Joseph P. Kennedy II and his son U.S. Representative **Joseph P. Kennedy III** chose to have their photograph taken at the John F. Kennedy birthplace, a National Historic Site, which was donated by the late president's mother, Rose Fitzgerald Kennedy, in 1966. The oldest son of Robert and Ethel Kennedy, as well as the first-born grandson of Rose and Joseph P. Kennedy, Sr., Joe served in the U.S. House of Representatives from 1987 to 1999. Joe founded the Citizens Energy Corporation in 1979 and returned to running the not-for-profit energy company after he left political office. The elder Kennedy's tenure in Congress included working on immigration issues and the Northern Ireland peace process. When he was elected to Congress in 2012, Joe III resumed the run of having a Kennedy family member in public office—a streak that spanned from 1947 until Representative Patrick J. Kennedy's term ended in 2011. The Kennedy historic site at 83 Beals Street in Brookline is located in the representative's district (the Massachusetts 4th) and near his home with wife, Lauren. Joe attended Stanford University with his twin brother, Matthew, and studied law at Harvard. He served in the Peace Corps, stationed in the Dominican Republic, and worked as an assistant district attorney in Middlesex and the Cape and Island's District Attorneys' Offices. In his first term, Joe has been a strong voice for equality and social justice issues and funding for workplace training and education.

Ed Markey

U.S. Senator **Ed Markey** says the spirit of his Irish immigrant heritage has informed his four-decade career of public service. Ed, who is Irish on both sides of his family, served in the U.S. House of Representatives for 37 years, until he was elected to the Senate in a special election in June 2013. Ed has focused his legislative efforts on fairness, justice, and opportunity for all Americans and people worldwide. Whether the issue is climate change, clean energy, safeguarding privacy, nuclear nonproliferation, investor protection, or preserving an open Internet that spurs competition and job creation, Ed says he is guided by a deep commitment to improving peoples' lives. His paternal great-grandfather emigrated from Co. Monaghan in 1858, while both his maternal grandparents left Co. Kerry for Massachusetts in the early 20th century. A graduate of Boston College and Boston College Law School, Ed served as state representative for two terms in the Massachusetts State House, representing Malden and Melrose.

Funeral of Lieutenant Stephen F. Minehan

More than 8,000 firefighters, some from as far away as Ontario and Los Angeles, lined up outside St. Brendan's Church in Dorchester alongside family, friends, and city officials to pay their respects as the casket of Lieutenant **Stephen F. Minehan**, who was killed trying to rescue two other Boston firefighters, was placed atop Engine 33. It was a hot day on June 24, 1994, when the Boston Fire Department crews came from all over the city to battle a nine-alarm fire that raged through a warehouse on the Charlestown pier. When two firefighters were trapped, Steve ran in to save them. The firefighters were rescued, but Steve died in the fire. Steve's Boylston Street firehouse, home to Engine 33 and Ladder 15, would face tragedy again in March 2014 when Lieutenant Edward J. Walsh and firefighter Michael Kennedy died in a nine-alarm fire on Beacon Street in the Back Bay. Steve was the third generation of his family to serve in the Boston Fire Department. His grandfather came from Ireland in 1899 and joined the department a year later, ultimately rising to the rank of district chief. Steve's father is credited with helping to save nine people in the 1942 Cocoanut Grove fire that claimed 492 lives. In 2012, Steve's son Joseph, a Boston firefighter, was promoted to lieutenant. Steve's widow, Kathleen, has worked over the years with the families of other firefighters who have died in the line of duty. On June 24, 2014, the Minehan family and others gathered in Charlestown at the site of the fire, now marked by a plaque at the Residence Inn Marriott Boston Harbor on Tudor Wharf, to recognize the 20th anniversary of Steve's death and raise money for area charities.

Angie and Dennis Lehane

"Most of my books are odes to sections of one city," author **Dennis Lehane** told a television crew about his fascination with Boston, his hometown. Dennis, who was being interviewed for a program called *Irish Writers in America*, spoke about being an Irish Catholic in Dorchester in the 1970s. "I grew up in an immigrant culture," he said, noting that his former street in St. Margaret's Parish is now populated mostly with people who emigrated from Cambodia. Dennis was photographed with his wife, **Angie**, an optometrist, while the two were at a Boston area event in 2013. He is the youngest of five children born to Michael, a foreman at Sears, Roebuck, & Co., and Ann (Folan) Lehane, a homemaker. Michael was born in Drimoleague, Co. Cork, the 17th of 18 children, and raised on his family's farm in Clonakilty. Ann emigrated from Connemara. Dennis is the author of a dozen books, three of which—*Mystic River*, *Gone Baby Gone*, and *Shutter Island*—were turned into movies.

David F. Powers

David F. Powers often described himself as "just a newsboy who met a president," but he served as John F. Kennedy's personal aide and grew to be the president's close friend and confidant. Dave and other Boston Irish-Americans in the president's inner circle were referred to as the "Irish Murphia," but never within earshot of President Kennedy. Shown here with models of statues that were collected for the 1979 opening of the John F. Kennedy Library and Museum at Columbia Point in Dorchester, Dave left Washington in 1965 to join the then-proposed library as a curator. "Jack loved Dave Powers like a brother, and so did all of us in the Kennedy family," Senator Edward M. Kennedy told *The Boston Globe* when Dave died in 2007. Dave was the son of Irish immigrants from Co. Cork who settled in Charlestown. His father died when Dave was two, and, at age 10, he sold newspapers in the Charlestown Navy Yard to support his family.

Thomas P. and Shelly O'Neill

Thomas P. O'Neill III and his wife, **Shelly**, arrive at the annual dinner for the American Ireland Fund, an organization they both actively support. Tom is the CEO of O'Neill and Associates, a lobbying, public relations and government affairs firm. He was the lieutenant governor in Governor Michael S. Dukakis's first administration and during Governor King's term and was previously a state representative. He is the son of the late Congressman Thomas P. "Tip" O'Neill, Jr., who served as speaker of the U.S. House of Representatives from 1977 to 1987. Tom, like his father, attended Boston College and went on to study at the John F. Kennedy School of Government at Harvard. The O'Neill family is from North Cambridge, where they settled after leaving Ireland. In 2012, Tom and his siblings led a large family delegation to Buncrana, Co. Donegal, near where Tom's great-grandmother lived, for a celebration led by Irish Taoiseach Enda Kenny, marking the O'Neill family's history in the region.

Robert H. and Claudina Quinn

Robert H. Quinn met his beloved wife, Claudina, on a blind date. They soon married and moved into the Quinn family home in Dorchester. While raising four now-successful children, the couple opened their Milton home for numerous causes over the years before returning to Dorchester and trading partygoers for their seven grandchildren. Claudina's family came to Massachusetts from Ireland after the famine, and she grew up in Milford. Bob's mother came from Roscommon and his father from Galway. Bob, the first in his family to go to college, earned scholarships to Boston College High School, Boston College and Harvard Law School. He started his fulfilling political career in 1957, winning a seat from his Dorchester neighborhood in the state House of Representatives, where he rose to become speaker. He was proud of his accomplishments, which included the creation of the University of Massachusetts Boston, and the passage of the Quinn Bill, an effort to professionalize police forces through educational incentives. After serving as the state's attorney general, he left public office in 1975 and founded the law firm of Quinn & Morris with his former assistant James T. Morris. He passed away in 2014. Claudina has maintained an active charitable career. She was a longtime board member of St. Margaret's Hospital in Dorchester where, as chairwoman, she shepherded the hospital's transition to St. Mary's Women's and Infant's Center, which now serves women, teens and children in crisis. Among her many other philanthropic endeavors, Claudina served on the board and was later chairwoman for the Cardinal Cushing School and Training Center in Hanover, which was founded to empower those with special needs. Of all their accomplishments, the Quinns consider the success of the University of Massachusetts Boston and its enrollment of immigrants from more than 140 countries to be their greatest legacy.

Judge George A. O'Toole, Jr.

U.S. District Court Chief Judge **Patti B. Saris** presided over a different kind of ceremony at the Moakley Courthouse in South Boston when the portrait for U.S. District Court Judge **George A. O'Toole, Jr.** was unveiled before a packed courtroom. A Worcester native, George attended Boston College and Harvard Law School and was a partner at the Boston law firm Hale and Dorr before working as a Boston Municipal Court associate justice. He later served as an associate justice in Massachusetts Superior Court for five years. When George was nominated by President Clinton for the U.S. District Court post, *The Boston Globe* correctly predicted he would sail through the process. George's previous appointments had been made by political rivals Governors King and Dukakis. George's family traces its roots to the Ireland counties of Mayo and Cork.

Michael Patrick MacDonald

"Being a storyteller is my inheritance," says **Michael Patrick MacDonald**. "All my life, whether on my childhood street corners of Old Colony Project or at a typical 'kitchen racket' or pub séisiun my mother presided over with her accordion, telling stories in between reels, the story—and one's ability to tell it—has been central to our identities, our worldview, our strength and resilience." Michael attributes the most important aspects of who he is, a storyteller and a social justice activist, to his Irish heritage. "Whether 'in the blood' or not," he says, "these two most important things in the world to me were certainly passed down by the people who raised me." One of 11, Michael grew up in South Boston during the busing riots of the 1970s, saw the reign of Whitey Bulger, and lost four siblings to poverty and violence. He transformed his grief by working against violence and substance abuse and for social justice, and, in the aftermath, he wrote the memoir *All Souls: A Family Story From Southie*, a *New York Times*' best seller that has been assigned in some 500 schools and colleges across the country.

John J. Carroll

At 86, **John J. Carroll** has nothing left to prove, but his internal Irish spring hasn't wound down enough for him to stop working full-time as the general manager of the town of Norwood, a post he has held for 36 years. One hundred-percent Irish and 100-percent extrovert, the Milton resident has also served on the board of the MWRA since 1985—so long, in fact, that the agency named a $300-million water treatment plant in Marlborough after him. He can be seen most Sundays in his regular ushering role in the balcony at Park Street Church in downtown Boston. "My faith is very important to me," he says. His parents, Elizabeth and John J. Carroll, were both Irish immigrants from Co. Waterford. John is the father of 18 children, ranging in age from 40 to 60; 42 grandchildren; and five great-grandchildren. "I feel blessed that I've been able to raise, or partially raise, 18 kids," says John. He and his first wife, Marilyn, started with six children. After her death in 1976, he married Penny Martin, who had eight of her own—and then they adopted four more. John also served as the commissioner of the state Department of Public Works under Governor Michael Dukakis from 1975 through 1978.

Monica and James P. McIntyre

Over at the Heights, **James P. McIntyre** might be "Mr. Boston College," but he and **Monica (Flatley) McIntyre**, his wife of more than 50 years, have titles that they are more proud of: parents of three sons and three daughters and grandparents of 16. Jim, a senior vice president at Boston College, met Monica at the Jesuit university where they both worked. He says he was brought up by his "parents to value family and church and to be thrifty and work hard." Jim's father, Peter, was born in 1902 in Co. Cork, and his mother, Ann F. Halloran, was born four years later in Co. Galway. Both immigrated to Boston in the mid-1920s. By day, Jim worked a string of jobs to pay for his evening classes at Boston College, where he earned a bachelor's degree in six years and, later, master's and doctoral degrees. Monica's father, Patrick James Flatley, was born in Ballyhaunis in Co. Mayo. He immigrated to America at 18, was drafted into the U.S. Army, and was headed to the front lines in 1919 just as World War I ended. He went back to Ireland to court Peggy Kelly of Claremorris, Co. Mayo. They left Ireland on their wedding day in 1926 and came to Boston, where Peggy's brother lived. They later bought a home in Brookline, where they raised Monica and her five sisters and seven brothers.

Daniel J. Mahoney

As a boy, Reverend **Daniel J. Mahoney** could not decide whether he wanted to be a priest or a firefighter. He found a way to do both. The chaplain for the Boston Fire Department for nearly 50 years, Father Dan has been a priest for nearly 60 years. He was photographed with the 2013 department academy class. During his time working with the fire department, Father Dan has provided comfort to the families of 51 Boston firefighters who have died in the line of duty: from fires, accidents, or illness. Most recently, he performed last rites for Boston firefighter Michael R. Kennedy, who, along with Lieutenant Edward J. Walsh, Jr., was killed in a Back Bay fire in March 2014. A first-generation Irish American, Father Dan was raised in Haverhill, where his father opened a neighborhood hardware store after saving enough money working on the docks of East Boston, and as a pipe fitter and a boilermaker. The pastor of St. Francis de Sales Church in Charlestown, Father Dan has also been a leader in his community, reaching out to new immigrants and others trying to make a better life.

John P. and Maureen Connolly

John P. Connolly and his wife, **Maureen P. (Rohan) Connolly**, unabashedly promote the art of Ireland, especially dramatic landscapes of the "vanishing countryside," says Maureen. Their Aisling Gallery has been the home to painter Vincent Crotty from Kanturk, Co. Cork, since shortly after it opened on Lincoln Street in Hingham, Massachusetts, in 1989. "He certainly will be known as one of Ireland's great artists," Maureen says. "In his oil paintings, he has the ability to paint light that one cannot forget—it's that emotional connection to Ireland's haunting images of its landscapes and people." Other Irish artists who are shown at Aisling—the

Gaelic word for dream—include Eugene Conlon, Syra Larkin, Daniel Gaudette, Edmund Sullivan, Kathryn Duprex, and John Skelton. For the Connollys, the gallery is an extension of their heritage. John's father emigrated from Moycullen, Co. Galway, and his mother from Curry, Co. Sligo. He graduated from Boston Latin School and Boston College. Maureen emigrated with her twin sister, Teresa, from Castlegregory, Co. Kerry to Boston in October 1960. She received a bachelor's degree from Harvard University's Extension School. The Connollys also use the gallery and frame shop to host Irish cultural events throughout the year.

Winnie Henry

When Haiti was struck with a devastating earthquake, **Winnie Henry** was spurred into action. This Milton mother of seven joined with Pat "Doc" Walsh and held "Irish Hearts for Haiti," an event that raised money to benefit children of the Caribbean nation. Now called "Irish Hearts for Orphans," Winnie's project has grown and is now part of NPH International, which has provided critical support to more than 1 million people since the 2010 earthquake. Born in Brighton, Winnie's family came to the United States from Co. Galway—Ballinasloe and Loughrea. Her late husband, Noel, the renowned leader of Noel Henry's Irish Showband, is still remembered for his renditions of *The Old Claddagh Ring* and *Lady of Knock* some 20 years after his death. Noel was born in Balla, Co. Mayo, and came to America in 1969. He founded the travel company Noel Henry Tours, which often included musical performances. His band continues to perform and now counts Caroline Henry Brennan, Winnie and Noel's oldest daughter among its members.

John McDonough and Michael D. O'Neill

John McDonough, the interim superintendent of the Boston Public School system and its 56,000 students, and **Michael D. O'Neill**, chairman of the Boston School Committee, are both natives of Jamaica Plain. John (left) started with the Boston Public Schools in 1973 as a temporary clerk, was named CFO in 1996, and was appointed interim superintendent in May 2013. A lifelong resident of Boston, John graduated magna cum laude with a bachelor's degree in political science and an MBA from Boston College. His father's family came from Co. Galway. John's mother's family emigrated from Co. Sligo. His grandfather was John P. Higgins, a U.S. Representative and the United States judge on the War Crimes Tribunal in Japan. Michael O'Neill, along with his four siblings, first lived in the same home that his grandfather John H. O'Neill, Sr. built next door to Mayor James Michael Curley's famous "house with the shamrock shutters" on the Jamaicaway. His family emigrated from the family farm in Ferlihanes, Rossmore, Co. Cork. Michael, who is executive vice president at 451 Marketing, graduated from Boston Latin, where this photograph was taken. He went on to earn his bachelor's degree from Boston College and receive an MBA from Babson College. In 2008, he was appointed to the school committee and served as chairman for two years.

Robert K. Coughlin

There was no doubt for **Robert K. Coughlin**, president and CEO of the Massachusetts Biotechnology Council, that, when it came time to pick a location for his photograph to be taken, he'd be "right outside one of the labs where they are doing some of the most innovative research on cystic fibrosis," Bob says of the work being done in Kendall Square where the council is based. Bob's 12-year-old son Bobby, the third of three children with his wife, Christine, has cystic fibrosis, and Bob has made it his mission to support companies doing cutting-edge research in all fields. "It brings my worlds together," says Bob. "The Irish have a higher incidence of CF, so I believe we have to work harder to help stop this." A former state representative, Bob also served in the Patrick Administration in economic development. He is a graduate of the Massachusetts Maritime Academy and is a lieutenant in the U.S. Naval Reserve. Bob's family emigrated from Co. Roscommon and Co. Cork several generations ago and ultimately made their way to the Boston area.

Senator Thomas P. Kennedy

Few people have dedicated themselves to their community more than state Senator **Thomas P. Kennedy** has to Brockton, his lifelong hometown. The youngest of four children born to Robert and Mary (Cruise) Kennedy, Tom lives in the house his grandparents bought before World War I. (For many years Tom shared the house with his mother, who died in November 2011 at 101 years old.) His maternal grandparents came to America from Co. Mayo and Co. Roscommon. His father's relatives arrived in North America via Nova Scotia. After graduating from Cardinal Spellman High School, Tom entered the Missionary Oblates of Mary Immaculate in New York to begin his studies to become a priest. In 1971, he had an accident that left him a quadriplegic and confined to a wheelchair. Tom's career in politics started with a job offer from Brockton Mayor David Crosby, which led to his running for City Council. He later topped nine other candidates for state representative and held that position until 2008, when he ran for—and won—a seat in the state Senate.

Richard F. Jr. and Ann Marie Connolly

Financial industry publications have ranked Morgan Stanley Managing Director **Richard F. Connolly, Jr.** as one of the top stockbrokers in the country, but Dick has never forgotten where he came from. Growing up in Woburn, Dick excelled as a golfer and was awarded an Ouimet Scholarship to attend the College of the Holy Cross. He now serves on the board of the Francis Ouimet Scholarship Fund and has helped raised millions so that others can receive a college education. Dick and his wife, **Ann Marie**, who also graduated from Holy Cross, have three sons. They support a number of charities, including their alma mater, and met at a President's Council dinner at the Worcester college. A native of Providence, Rhode Island,

Ann Marie earned a master's of education from Boston University. Dick's family comes from Co. Galway, and his maternal grandmother emigrated from Pontoon, Co. Mayo. "Being Irish means I have a responsibility. I have a responsibility to succeed—because my ancestors did not have the opportunities to do so," he told *Irish America* when he was selected for their 2014 list of the "Wall Street 50." Dick is on the Board of Overseers of the Boston Symphony Orchestra. He has used his golf prowess to benefit charities, including the Children's Medical Research Foundation in Dublin, Ireland, and has chaired the foundation's annual golf tournament for the last 30 years.

Edward J. King, William M. Bulger, Tom O'Neill and Peter O'Neill

Governor **Edward J. King** (near left) was sworn in as the 66th governor of Massachusetts by Senate President **William M. Bulger** (center) before a packed legislative chamber on January 4, 1979. One of a line of 20th–century Irish-American governors, Ed defeated incumbent Michael Dukakis in 1978 to gain the corner office at the State House. He was previously executive director of the Massachusetts Port Authority. Ed left office in 1983 after he lost the Democratic nomination to Dukakis, who went on to reclaim the governorship in the 1982 election. Born in Chelsea, Ed grew up in East Boston at a time when the neighborhood was transitioning from being home to Irish immigrants to that of those emigrating from Italy. Ed enrolled at Boston College, where he excelled at football, and, after graduation, he played for three seasons as a lineman for the Buffalo Bills and the Baltimore Colts. Ed died in September 2006 at age 81. William Bulger was first elected to the House of Representatives in 1960, representing South Boston. Ten years later, he was elected to the state Senate and served as president from 1978 until 1996, the longest-serving president in the Senate's history. **Thomas P. O'Neill III** (back left) was lieutenant governor in Governor Dukakis's first term and also served with Governor King. **Peter O'Neill** (back right) was a clerk with the House Speaker's office at the time of the inauguration. Peter, who also worked as chief of staff during Speaker David M. Bartley's tenure, is a lawyer with the Boston firm Quinn & Morris. No relation to the former lieutenant governor, Peter is part of the same family as the late Boston City Councilor Albert "Dapper" O'Neil, but spells his name differently. His family emigrated from Kerry and Cork.

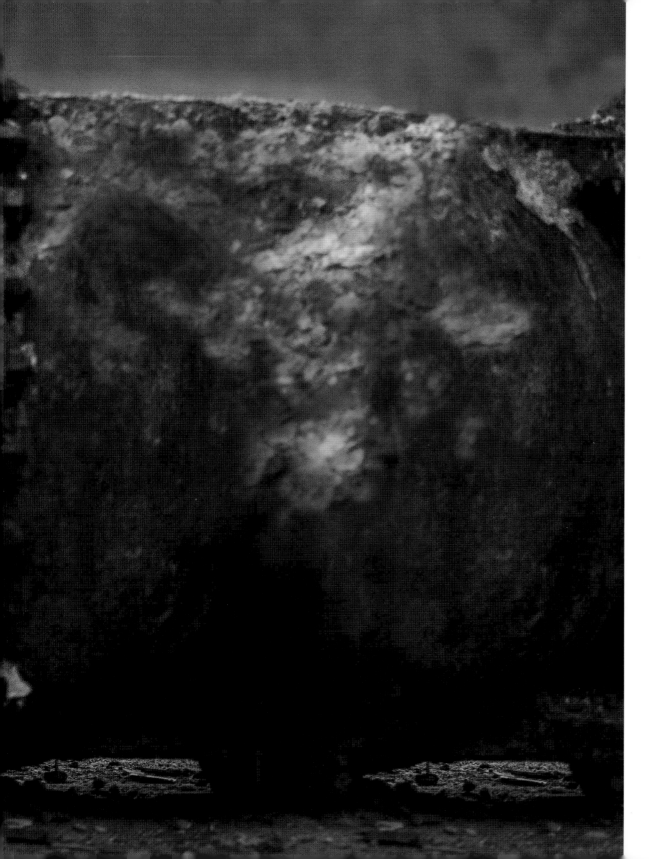

John P. Sullivan, Jr.

John P. Sullivan, Jr., chief engineer for the Boston Water and Sewer Commission, represents the third generation of his family to serve the citizens of Boston. John has worked for the city's water and sewer departments since 1972. John grew up in West Roxbury, as one of eight siblings—including two who also work in the water and sewer department as had their father, John P. Sullivan, and grandfather, Daniel M. Sullivan. The Sullivans arrived in America in 1849 from Co. Cork. John's mother's ancestors came to Boston from Cahir, Co. Tipperary and Kiltyclogher, Co. Leitrim. John attended Boston Latin and received a bachelor's degree in civil engineering from University of Massachusetts Amherst. He is photographed with a pipe that is part of a valve used to control water flow. Installed in 1888 in Dorchester, the 125-year-old pipe system was reconditioned and has been placed back into service.

Christopher E. McIntosh

Christopher E. McIntosh says that his heritage is "like an amazing smoothly blended whiskey"—a mix of Scottish and Irish traditions with his family tree growing from Inverness-shire. Chris is chief marketing officer at Baystate Financial and formerly was president and publisher of the award-winning *Boston Business Journal*. During Chris's tenure at the news operation, which includes *Mass High Tech*, newsletters, and other business-sector content, the *Boston Business Journal* saw its online platform grow to millions of page-views per month. A seasoned sales executive with a background in business communications, marketing, operational management, and digital publishing, Chris uses his business acumen in a philanthropic way and oversaw the donation of nearly a million dollars of media support and cash to local charities. Chris serves on nine boards of Boston area nonprofits, including the Boston Irish Business Association, which is committed to retaining and strengthening the Boston business community's connections with Ireland and Northern Ireland.

The Cleary Brothers

The story of **Robert** and **William J. Cleary**, **Jr.**'s (right) Cambridge childhood goes something like this: they grew up so close to Harvard that their Irish-American family had to move every time the university's campus was expanded. They would soon be part of Harvard where Bill ('56) set hockey records that stood only until his younger brother Bob ('58) led the squad. "We didn't have any indoor rinks when we were kids," Bill told WBUR-FM's Bob Oakes. "We had to learn on the Charles River—I did because I grew up in Cambridge—on Spy Pond in Arlington and all these little places in Lexington and Concord.

We'd find ice wherever it was." The brothers are best known for leading the U.S. hockey team for the first "Miracle on Ice" at the 1960 Winter Olympics in Squaw Valley, California. At the height of the Cold War, the U.S. team defeated the Soviet team for the first time and went on to capture the first gold medal that the United States had ever won in hockey. Bill returned to Harvard in 1971 to coach the men's hockey team for more than 20 years; there he led the team to more than a dozen titles, including the NCAA championship in 1989.

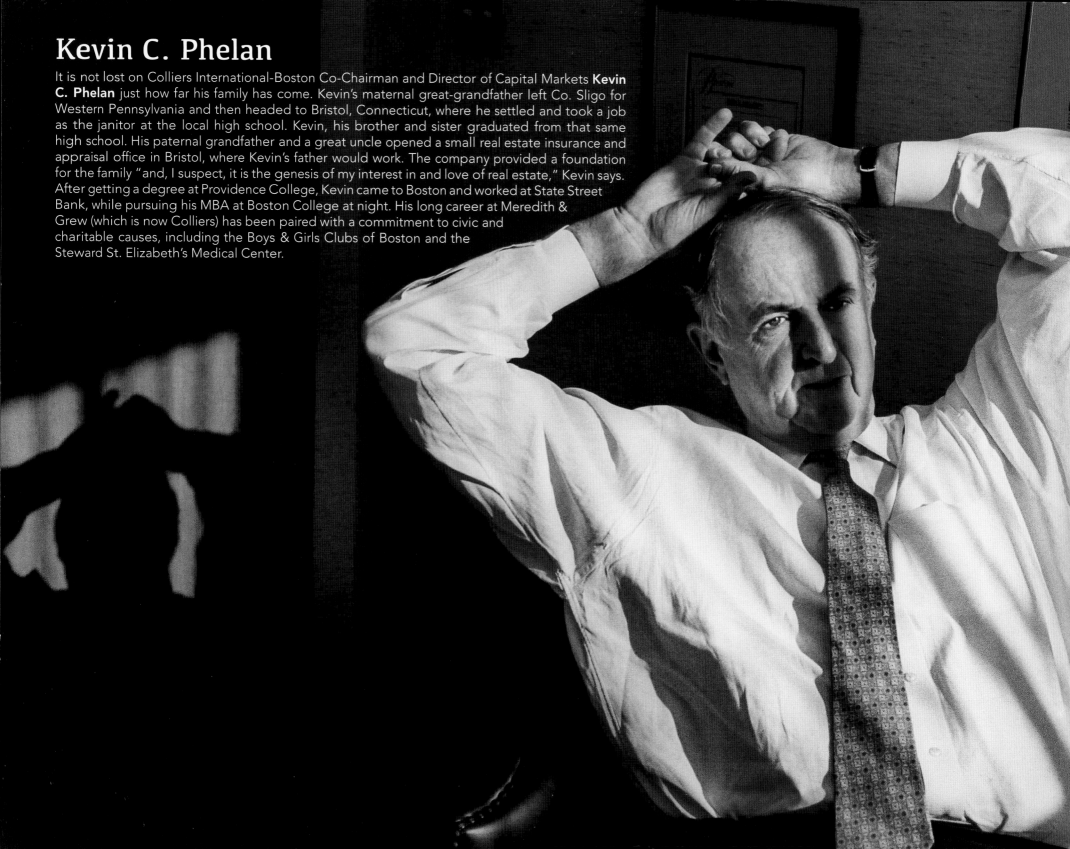

Kevin C. Phelan

It is not lost on Colliers International-Boston Co-Chairman and Director of Capital Markets **Kevin C. Phelan** just how far his family has come. Kevin's maternal great-grandfather left Co. Sligo for Western Pennsylvania and then headed to Bristol, Connecticut, where he settled and took a job as the janitor at the local high school. Kevin, his brother and sister graduated from that same high school. His paternal grandfather and a great uncle opened a small real estate insurance and appraisal office in Bristol, where Kevin's father would work. The company provided a foundation for the family "and, I suspect, it is the genesis of my interest in and love of real estate," Kevin says. After getting a degree at Providence College, Kevin came to Boston and worked at State Street Bank, while pursuing his MBA at Boston College at night. His long career at Meredith & Grew (which is now Colliers) has been paired with a commitment to civic and charitable causes, including the Boys & Girls Clubs of Boston and the Steward St. Elizabeth's Medical Center.

Thomas H. O'Connor

Thomas H. O'Connor wrote the book on Boston—several of them. The Boston College professor and historian wrote 10 books that are must-reads for anyone who wants to understand the city. When Tom died in May 2012 at age 89, *The Boston Globe* wrote that he was "the unofficial dean of Boston history." In addition to his six-decade career at Boston College, he taught at the Harvard Extension School. Born into an Irish-Catholic family in South Boston, Tom worked at the Boston Public Library while a student at Boston Latin School. His book *Bibles, Brahmins, and Bosses: A Short History of Boston* grew out of a library lecture series, and *Fitzpatrick's Boston, 1846-1866*, would follow. "It introduced me to some of the background history of the Irish. It made me realize, 'There is stuff in this,'" he told *The Globe* in a 2002 interview. He served on the Massachusetts Archives Commission, the National Bicentennial Commission, and was awarded the Eire Society of Boston Gold Medal in 1999.

Kip Tiernan

When **Kip Tiernan** died in 2011 at age 85, *The Boston Globe* wrote that Kip "directly or indirectly…may have touched more lives of the poor in the Commonwealth than anyone else in the past four decades." Kip, who founded Rosie's Place in 1974 and was part of the creation of a number of programs and agencies, put a face on the problem of homeless people in Boston and gave a voice to women in the region who wouldn't otherwise be heard. The daughter of George, a tavern owner, and Anna (Farrell) Tiernan, Kip was raised in West Haven, Connecticut. Her parents died when she was young, and she was raised by her grandmother. According to Beth Healy, who is working on a book and a screenplay about the remarkable woman, Kip was an accomplished pianist who would play *Danny Boy* for her classmates at the Lauralton Hall Catholic Girls School in Connecticut.

Diddy and John Cullinane

John Cullinane and his wife, **Diddy**, have long been active in civic, social, and cultural causes in the United States, Ireland, and Northern Ireland. Diddy traces her roots to Co. Galway, and the Aran Islands, and Nova Scotia before her relatives settled in Dorchester, where she was born. John's parents immigrated to the United States in 1929 from Dunmore East, Co. Waterford, and settled in Arlington, Massachusetts, where John was born and raised. He graduated from Northeastern, where he later served as a trustee, and founded Cullinet Software, Inc., one of the first companies to specialize in computer software products. After selling his company in 1989, John and his wife focused on their civic and philanthropic work. She has long been supportive of the Boston Symphony Orchestra and created Black & White Boston, which supported community programs and funded scholarships for inner-city youths. John was the first chairman of the Boston Public Library Foundation, and Diddy created its first gala, causing a stir when tickets for the 1993 fete were an unheard-of $1,000 a person. John was the first president of the John F. Kennedy Library Foundation and the founder of the Friends of Belfast. He also participated in Taoiseach Bertie Ahern's 1998 Ireland-America Economic Advisory Board mission to Ireland, and in other work to support economic prosperity and peace in Ireland and Northern Ireland.

Lisa Hughes and Carolyn M. Casey

WBZ-TV news anchor **Lisa Hughes** (left) was working near the finish line of the Boston Marathon in 2013 when the two bombs exploded killing three. Her friend and sister-in-law **Carolyn M. Casey** was running in her first Boston Marathon and just a couple of blocks up Boylston Street as the second bomb went off. Both were unhurt, and Lisa and her WBZ television and radio colleagues would be recognized for their coverage with duPont-Columbia and Peabody awards. Lisa's family is from counties Cork and Sligo, and her maternal grandfather, Dennis Hurley, a New York City fire captain, was second-generation Irish. Lisa supports a number of Boston nonprofits: Big Sister Association of Greater Boston, Pan-Mass Challenge, and Boston Ballet. Carolyn is founder and executive director of Project 351, a nonprofit youth service organization that gives an eighth grader from every city and town in the Commonwealth a year of leadership and transformational service. The Caseys trace their heritage back to the Ireland counties of Roscommon, Cork, and Leitrim. The family settled in the Irish boroughs of Jamaica Plain, Mission Hill, West Roxbury, and Taunton. Carolyn's parents and maternal grandparents were all educators, and from them she "gained my passionate belief that every young person has unlimited potential and deserves unconditional love."

Samuel H. Kennedy and Thomas B. Kennedy

The Reverend **Thomas B. Kennedy**'s paternal grandparents William and Hannah Kennedy arrived in America in November 1922, having come from a townland near Ballybay, Co. Monaghan, in the newly established Free State. They left because of the fighting between Protestants and Catholics. Tom's father, Robert George Kennedy, was age 12 when his family was processed through Ellis Island after a 12-day ship passage at sea. They settled in Sherman, Connecticut, on a small farm. "Dad was a hard worker and a man of impeccable integrity; his word was his contract," Tom says. After college, Tom and his wife, Joanna, headed to the Episcopal Theological School in Cambridge, Massachusetts, as he prepared for the ministry. He was ordained a priest in the Episcopal Church in 1969, served as associate rector of Trinity Church in Copley Square for 15 years and as dean of the Cathedral Church of St. Paul for five years. In retirement, he serves as chairman of the Board of Sherrill House, a 196-bed rehabilitation and extended care facility in Jamaica Plain, and as president of the Boston Episcopal Charitable Society, the oldest charitable society in New England, established by the King of England in 1724. **Samuel H. Kennedy**, the oldest son and middle child of Tom and Joanna's three children, is a graduate of Brookline High School and Trinity College. He was a college intern for the New York Yankees and later worked for the San Diego Padres. In 2002, Sam joined the new ownership of the Red Sox and is now chief operating officer of the Boston Red Sox and president of Fenway Sports Management, a wholly owned marketing company of Fenway Sports Group. The two were photographed in the stands of Fenway Park.

Kenny Young

Kenny Young knows Boston from the outside in. Best known from his reign as doorman at the original Ritz-Carlton hotel on Arlington Street, Kenny carries natural Irish hospitality and warmth to his role as chauffeur and owner of the limousine and concierge service company Kenny's Car, based in Weston, Massachusetts. Kenny's Irish heritage is traced back through his grandparents William Young and Agnes McDowell, who immigrated to Boston from Ireland at the dawn of the 20th century. Being able to walk with kings and nobility comes straight from Kenny's early forebear, Sir Francis Bryan, a 14th-century poet, translator, soldier, and diplomat who served as an adviser and courtier to King Henry VIII and married Lady Joan Fitzgerald. Kenny lights up when he talks about his Irish heritage: "That would be the ultimate test of hospitality and service—sharing and driving a carriage with King Henry VIII, you'd *really* have to keep your head!"

Judge William T. Hogan, Jr.

Back when retired Dedham District Court Judge **William T. Hogan, Jr**. was a young ace pitcher for the Jeveli's Restaurant team in the local park league, East Boston's transition from being a primarily Irish-American neighborhood to becoming the home of new Italian immigrant families was already under way. And the roll call of the Jeveli's sponsored team—"Marmo, Poto, Basile, Festa…and Hogan"—usually got a few laughs, William remembers. While he was a student at St. Mary's School, William met and became friends with Edward J. King, who served as governor from 1979 to 1983. During that time, William served in a series of state posts, including chairman of the Parole Board and secretary of Human Services. William's family came to America from Co. Cork and Dungarvan, Co. Waterford. He has been married to Dorothea A. Shea since 1952, and the couple is parents to 10 children, five of whom, like their father, became lawyers, including Mary Hogan Sullivan, first justice of the Dedham District Court.

The Walsh Family

The story of **Eddie Walsh, Sr.**'s career in law enforcement now spans three generations. Eddie (second from left) was 91 when this photograph was taken. He joined the Boston Police Department in 1955 and served 32 years, retiring as deputy superintendent. His son **Eddie Walsh, Jr.** (far left) joined the department in 1978 and served for 33 years before retiring as a detective. Officer **Jeffrey Callahan**, (third from left) grandson of Eddie Sr., has been on the job since 2011 and works out of the District C-11 station in Dorchester, one of the department's largest districts. **James Walsh** (right), son of Eddie, Jr., also joined the department in 2011 and is assigned to the District B-2 station in Roxbury. James, who is wearing a black band on his badge in remembrance of a deceased family member, and his father are members of the Boston Police Gaelic Column of Pipes and Drums. Eddie Sr. was born and raised in South Boston and started his family there. He moved his wife and children to Dorchester—St. Brendan's Parish—in 1960 because he needed more room to accommodate his growing clan. Eddie Jr., is one of eight and also lived in St. Brendan's Parish, as does his son James. Eddie Sr.'s father hailed from Co. Tipperary, and his mother was from Co. Galway. They both came to Boston at the turn of the last century and met at the Irish dances held at Roxbury's Hibernian Hall around 1910.

The Lee Kennedy Family

Lee M. Kennedy, Sr. founded Lee Kennedy Co. in 1978, a construction company with notable projects including the John F. Kennedy Presidential Library and Museum at Columbia Point, MIT's Kresge Auditorium, and the Edward M. Kennedy Institute for the United States Senate, which is slated to open in 2015. Lee is shown in the photograph flanked by his two sons, **Lee Michael Kennedy** (left), the company's president and CEO, and **Eugene Kennedy**, vice president. Lee Sr. was born at St. Margaret's Hospital in Dorchester and the family lived on Gallivan Boulevard (St. Brendan's Parish), before moving to Milton. Lee Sr.'s paternal grandparents were born in Ireland and lived in Brooklyn, N.Y., before moving to Helen Street in Dorchester around the turn of the last century. Lee Sr.'s mother was raised in Brighton, and her father, who was from Ireland, was a motorman with the old Street Railway system. All three Kennedy men support area charities, including the Boys & Girls Clubs of Dorchester, College Bound Dorchester, Franciscan Hospital for Children, and the Francis Ouimet Scholarship Fund.

Paddy Grace and Jim O'Brien

When The Littlest Bar closed at the end of 2006, **Paddy Grace**, who came to the United States from Callan, Co. Kilkenny, looked to mythology, stating that, like the phoenix, the tiny pub would rise from the ashes. And it has, reopening on Broad Street as a larger bar and restaurant. The Littlest Bar, which operated on Province Street near Old City Hall, was never bigger than its name, with a city license that restricted the capacity to 38 people, including the staff. In fact, opening the door of the wee place would necessitate having the entire bar move. Paddy, an avid fisherman who loves to follow the hurling matches, has been the bar's proprietor since 1990. The Littlest Bar hosted politicians, lawyers, laborers, retailers, and financial services workers as they conversed while jockeying for just a little more room. Paddy is seen here talking to **Jim O'Brien**, the former president of the New England Chapter of the Ireland Chamber of Commerce in the United States. Jim, a former Boston College football player, is credited with bringing American college football to Ireland. More than 42,000 fans watched Boston College beat Army in 1988.

The Sullivan Family

The story of the Sullivan family in Cambridge politics is the story of the city's government since the Depression. A seat on the Cambridge City Council had been held by a member of the Sullivan family continuously from 1936 until 2007 and was affectionately called "The Sullivan Seat." Upholding the family's tradition is Middlesex Clerk of Courts **Michael A. Sullivan**, center, who served as city councilor from 1994 to 2007, including four years as mayor. Michael is shown standing in front of a portrait of his grandfather Michael "Mickey the Dude" Sullivan, a city councilor from 1936 to 1949 and father of the two men flanking Mickey and his namesake. Since this photograph was taken, Michael's portrait was added to the wall in the council meeting room, which is now called the Sullivan Chamber in the family's honor. In 2014, Mike lost the Democratic primary for the Middlesex District Attorney's office. At left is Michael's father, **Walter J. Sullivan**, a three-term mayor who served on the City Council from 1960 to 1994. He died in August 2014 at age 91. At right is Walter's brother **Edward J. Sullivan**, who served as city councilor from 1949 to 1960, including two years as mayor, and as Middlesex clerk of courts from 1959 to 2007. The family's service extended beyond elected office. One of Walter and Edward's three sisters was Mary McMorrow, who died in 2003, a city librarian who was known as the "first lady of Cambridge." The Sullivan family came from Kerry and, like so many from that county, settled in and around Harvard Square, where Mickey's aunt ran a boarding house.

The Hynes Family

John B. Hynes III (center) and his brother **Barry T. Hynes** continue a tradition begun by their grandfather Mayor John B. Hynes, whose time in office—the 1950s—was marked by tremendous growth and revitalization. They are also the sons of retired news anchor Jack Hynes. John is the owner and CEO of Boston Global Investors, a real estate development firm developing Seaport Square, where **John B. Hynes IV** (left) serves as a project manager. A 25-year veteran of Boston's commercial real estate sector, Barry is a partner with Cassidy Turley, where he advises some of the city's leading legal, financial, communications, and nonprofit organizations. The three are photographed outside Our Lady of Good Voyage, a Catholic chapel that was built in 1952 after Mayor Hynes made an appeal to Cardinal Cushing to open a church on the South Boston waterfront as a step toward making the rough-and-tumble area more welcoming. The church building is located on the Seaport Square property and is slated for demolition in 2015. A new chapel will be part of the new complex, and its construction will be overseen by John IV. The Hynes family's Boston story began when Mayor Hynes's father, Bernard, left Loughrea, Co. Galway, on board the steamship *Arizona*, arriving in New York in June 1888. Bernard settled in Roxbury and worked for 41 years on the Boston & Maine Railroad.

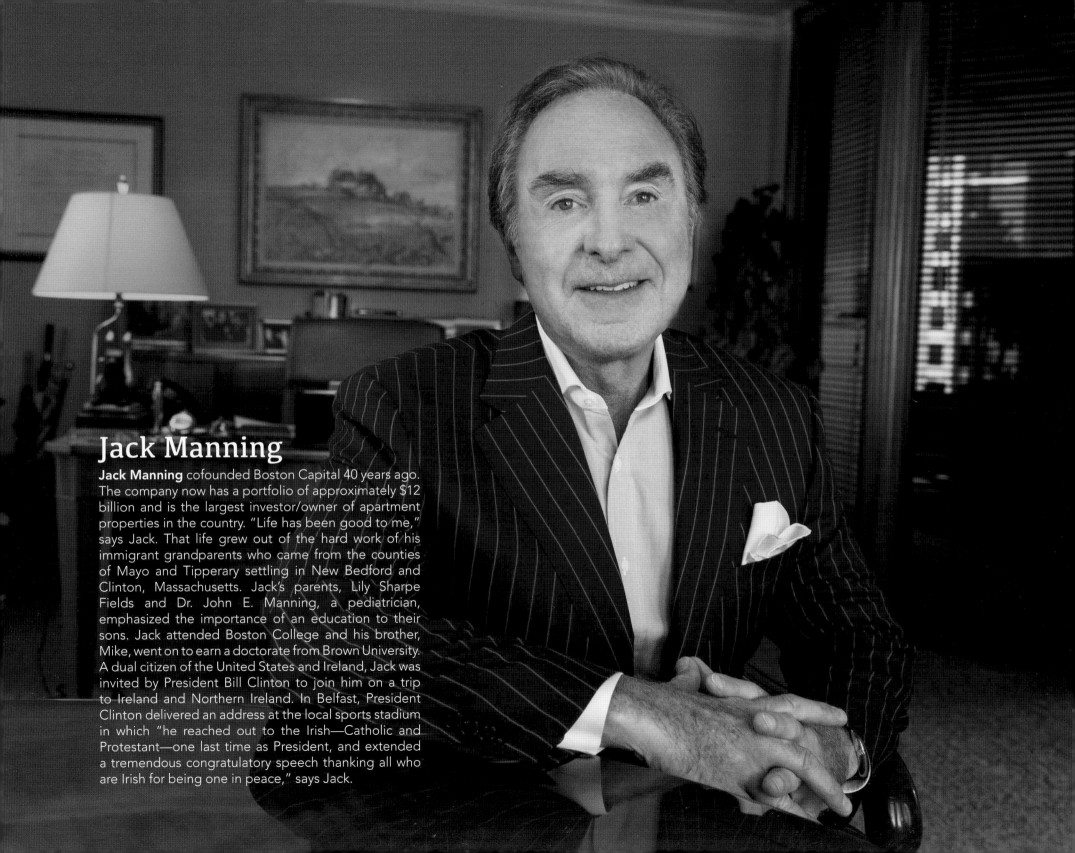

Jack Manning

Jack Manning cofounded Boston Capital 40 years ago. The company now has a portfolio of approximately $12 billion and is the largest investor/owner of apartment properties in the country. "Life has been good to me," says Jack. That life grew out of the hard work of his immigrant grandparents who came from the counties of Mayo and Tipperary settling in New Bedford and Clinton, Massachusetts. Jack's parents, Lily Sharpe Fields and Dr. John E. Manning, a pediatrician, emphasized the importance of an education to their sons. Jack attended Boston College and his brother, Mike, went on to earn a doctorate from Brown University. A dual citizen of the United States and Ireland, Jack was invited by President Bill Clinton to join him on a trip to Ireland and Northern Ireland. In Belfast, President Clinton delivered an address at the local sports stadium in which "he reached out to the Irish—Catholic and Protestant—one last time as President, and extended a tremendous congratulatory speech thanking all who are Irish for being one in peace," says Jack.

Christopher E. Goode

Christopher E. Goode is an indefatigable civic and community volunteer and is very active in a wide range of national and local civic and charitable organizations. He is a member of the boards of the John F. Kennedy Library Foundation and Camp Harbor View and is active with the Inner-City Scholarship Fund, and Boys & Girls Clubs of Boston. Chris is vice president global corporate affairs and chief public affairs officer for EMC Corporation, the global leader in information technology and one of the largest technology companies in the world, with more than 65,000 employees globally, including major facilities in Co. Cork. He serves on the boards of Associated Industries of Massachusetts, Greater Boston Chamber of Commerce and The New England Council. Chris was born and raised in the Savin Hill section of Dorchester and traces his heritage back to the Ireland counties of Cork, Galway, and Roscommon. Chris graduated from St. William's School in Dorchester, the Boston Latin School, and the College of the Holy Cross.

Steve Buckley

Longtime *Boston Herald* sports columnist **Steve Buckley** was born in Cambridge in 1956, as was his father, William Francis Buckley, in 1908. But when Steve dug a little deeper into his family's history, that's when things got murky. Family legend held that his grandfather William Avenas Buckley was born in Malden, Massachusetts, in 1862, but Steve couldn't find any records, so he quizzed an aging, beloved aunt. "You just mind your business," she told him. Steve discovered that his grandfather was actually born in Halifax, Nova Scotia, and that the family migrated to Cambridge in the 1880s. Steve's theory: Because these new Irish from Canada weren't much liked by the Irish who were already here, his ancestors simply told their new Cambridge neighbors they had moved from Malden. Steve maintains his ties to Cambridge; where each summer he holds the Oldtime Baseball Game, a celebration of baseball and a charity fundraiser he founded in 1994.

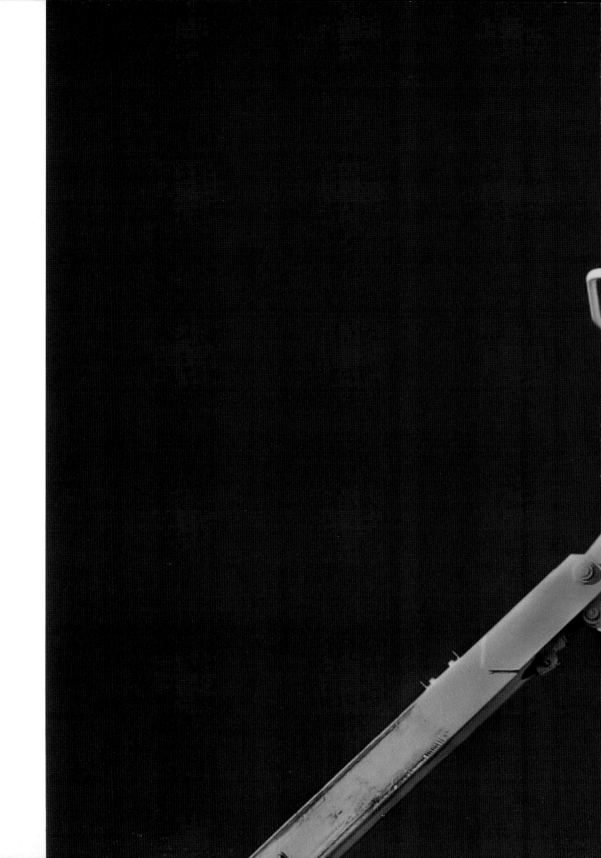

Bob Marr and Jack Shaughnessy

The cranes controlled by the companies of **Bob Marr** (left) and **Jack Shaughnessy** reach the heights of Boston's architecture and infrastructure, delivering people and construction materials daily to projects around—and sometimes under—the city. Two of the city's leading Irish-American business owners both quietly supported numerous charities. Bob is chairman of the Marr Companies, founded in 1898. In September 2014, Bob and his family gathered to award scholarships to 110 students attending Catholic schools as part of the Daniel F. Marr, Jr. Scholarship Endowment Fund of the Catholic Community Fund of the Archdiocese of Boston. Since its creation in 1992, the Marr endowment has awarded more than $900,000 in scholarships. In memory of their father, Bob and his brother Daniel F. Marr, Jr. also established the Boys & Girls Clubs of Dorchester as the Colonel Daniel Marr Boys & Girls Club in 1971. Jack was president of Shaughnessy & Ahern, founded in 1916, and a second company Shaughnessy Crane Service, which flourished under his leadership. When Jack died on November 27, 2013, the *Boston Irish Reporter* called him "a leading Catholic philanthropist." The Labouré Center in South Boston, The Rodman Ride for Kids, Catholic Charities of Boston, and My Brother's Keeper, a Christian ministry that delivers furniture and food to families in need, are among the organizations he supported.

James E. Kelly

The late City Councilor **James E. Kelly** was an old-school politician. Jimmy, who served 23 years on the City Council, including an unprecedented seven consecutive terms as its president, died on January 9, 2007, at age 66. Photographed outside Old City Hall—part of his district—Jimmy was an unflagging champion for his constituents. His family history traces back to the counties of Cork and Galway, Co. Armagh in Northern Ireland. A lifelong resident of South Boston, Jimmy first rose to prominence when Boston was under a federal court order to integrate its public schools.

Jimmy never changed his stance that the forced segregation hurt the city's school system and neighborhoods it was supposed to enhance. In 1999, Jimmy gave his support to a resolution to honor Martin Luther King, Jr., an act, City Councilor Charles C. Yancy told *The Boston Globe*, that "would have been unthinkable at the beginning of Mr. Kelly's career." In early 2007, the city named a bridge linking the South End to South Boston in honor of Jimmy.

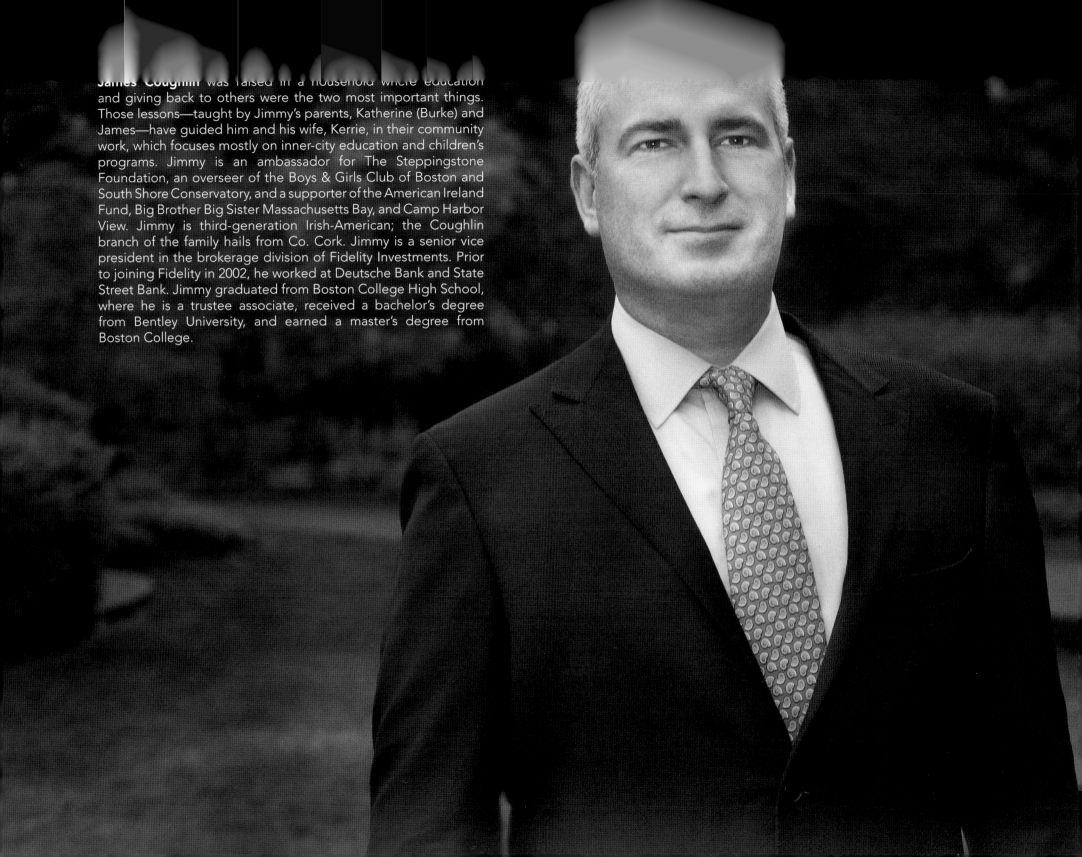

James Coughlin was raised in a household where education and giving back to others were the two most important things. Those lessons—taught by Jimmy's parents, Katherine (Burke) and James—have guided him and his wife, Kerrie, in their community work, which focuses mostly on inner-city education and children's programs. Jimmy is an ambassador for The Steppingstone Foundation, an overseer of the Boys & Girls Club of Boston and South Shore Conservatory, and a supporter of the American Ireland Fund, Big Brother Big Sister Massachusetts Bay, and Camp Harbor View. Jimmy is third-generation Irish-American; the Coughlin branch of the family hails from Co. Cork. Jimmy is a senior vice president in the brokerage division of Fidelity Investments. Prior to joining Fidelity in 2002, he worked at Deutsche Bank and State Street Bank. Jimmy graduated from Boston College High School, where he is a trustee associate, received a bachelor's degree from Bentley University, and earned a master's degree from Boston College.

Patrick and Peter Lee

Patrick Lee, left, and his brother **Peter** co-own some of the area's most popular restaurants—Grafton Street Pub & Grill, Temple Bar American Bistro, and PARK, in the former Redline Food and Drink space in Harvard Square—but their successful careers as restaurateurs trace back to the Brighton landmark The Irish Village. That authentic pub was opened in the early 1970s by their father, Peter Lee, Sr., a Co. Galway native. It was there that the brothers learned the business from the ground up; Peter first worked in the kitchen in the 1990s and later joined Patrick managing the front of the house. The brothers asked to be photographed in Dudley Square, Roxbury, once the heart of the social scene for young Irish and Irish Americans. They are standing just steps away from the Intercolonial Hall where Peter Sr. ran dances that drew hundreds of people to hear bands from across the Northeast and from Ireland. It is also the site where the Lee brothers' parents met. Even with their accomplishments, the brothers remember why they got into the business in the first place: to entertain people and build community.

Ed and Bill Forry

Ed Forry and his son, **Bill**, continue to uphold the long, proud tradition of newspaper publishers and editors who are members of the community they serve. Ed is founder and publisher of the *Boston Irish Reporter*, Boston's hometown journal of Irish culture. A lifelong resident of Dorchester and the originator of the OFD (Originally from Dorchester) designation, he is a "Double Eagle," having graduated from Boston College High School and Boston College. In 1983, Ed and his late wife, Mary Casey Forry, began publication of the *Dorchester Reporter*. It is considered the "newspaper of record," serving Boston's largest and most diverse neighborhood. Bill is publisher and managing editor of the *Dorchester Reporter*, the *Mattapan Reporter* and *Boston Haitian Reporter*, and editor of the *Boston Irish Reporter*. He has earned diplomas from Boston College High School and Boston College and holds a master's degree from the Harvard Kennedy School. The Forry family's roots are in the villages of the Irish counties of Sligo and Waterford, and Mary Casey's family came to Boston from Cork. In March 2014, Bill's wife, state Senator Linda Dorcena Forry, made Boston political history when she became the first woman, the first person of color, and the first politician from Dorchester to host the St. Patrick's Day political breakfast in South Boston.

Lawrence F. Reynolds, Sr.

The **Lawrence F. Reynolds, Sr**. story shown here is being told backwards, but it includes the most important thing in Larry's long and storied life—music. Larry, a virtuoso fiddler and considered by many to be the leader of Boston's Irish music community, was 80 years old when he died on October 3, 2012. This photograph was taken at the conclusion of the funeral Mass said in St. Jude Church in Waltham when dozens of musicians took out their instruments and played the traditional slow air *For Ireland I'd Not Tell Her Name* as the casket was carried out of the church. A master carpenter with Local 67 of the Carpenters Union in Dorchester, Larry grew up in Ahascragh, Co. Galway, and came to America in 1953. His wife, Phyllis, shared his love of music. Larry helped found the Boston chapter of Comhaltas Ceoltóirí Éireann, an international organization dedicated to preserving traditional Irish music, which is now called the Reynolds-Hanafin-Cooley branch.

Kathy Kiely

Kathy Kiely, president of The Ad Club, is proud of her Irish heritage. But when Kathy looks back on her 10 years at the helm of the Boston advertising industry association, which oversees 30 events every year, including the Hatch and Rosoff awards, she says she is most proud of her work on diversity. "We spread the message of bringing those new voices and diverse backgrounds to the boardroom," Kathy says. When asked about her Irish roots, Kathy remembers a tiny, black, button-up shoe that sat for many years on the mantel of the Medford home of her grandmother Madeline Meade Fitzpatrick. "[Madeline] was so upset about leaving Ireland as a child that she took off her other shoe and threw it into the ocean. Her mother told her, 'Well, you will just have to live in America with one shoe.'" Eventually, the Shannons, the Kielys, the Meades, and the Fitzpatricks all ended up married with children and living on Fells Avenue in Medford. "My father, Robert Emmet Kiely, said he used to watch my mother, June Fitzpatrick, walk to the bus every morning on her way to work and say: "I'm going to marry that girl."

ACKNOWLEDGEMENTS

There are many people I want to acknowledge for their support of this project. I am most grateful to my wife, Ginnie, for her unwavering affirmation and love; and the same to our wonderful children: Kerry Brett and Danny Gallagher; Megan and John Khayali; Liza and Tim Brett; and Erin Brett. Thank you, too, to my grandchildren: Morgan, Greyson, Hadley, Nora and a fifth on the way. To my siblings: Jim and his wife, Pattie; Mary McCarthy; Peggy McCobb; and Harry and his wife, Lucille. Your continuing love and support are invaluable. My mother, Mary Ann, and my brother Jack are no longer with us, but the way they lived their lives was, and is, an inspiration to me. They continue to show me the way.

I offer a most heartfelt thank-you to my friend and editor Carol Beggy, who spent countless hours researching information on the lives of the individuals in this book. Without her dedication, professionalism and patience, this volume would not have been possible. To my daughter Kerry Brett, who volunteered her time and expertise, and to my imaging technician and photo editor, Michael Petrocelli, thank you for all your hard work and time, and well done!

Special thanks go to my closest friends, David Mugar and R.J. Valentine, whose long-standing loyalty and encouragement contributed greatly to the making of this book. And to my late mentors, Don Bulman, Dan Sheehan, and Bob Dean, I think of you often and can never thank you enough. My utmost appreciation to: John Fish, Jack Connors, Joe Fallon, John Hailer, Joe Nolan, Bob Sheridan, Ken Quigley, Jr., Jim Rooney, Charlie Baker, Don Rodman, Kevin Phelan, Joe Milano, Rick Kelleher, Bob Davis, Mike Barnicle, Anne Finucane, Heather Campion, Peter Smyth, Mike Casey, Lisa Hughes, Bob McCarthy, Ruth and Gerard Adomunes, Bill Teuber, Kristan Fletcher, Justin Holmes, Lisa Tuite, and Katie Archambault.

To Annemarie Lewis Kerwin and Tom Mulvoy, thank you again and again for your friendship, encouragement, and unbridled enthusiasm for this project.

Much gratitude to my fellow photographers and circle of professional friends: Ted Gartland, Jim Wilson, Jim Bulman, Stan Grossfeld, David Ryan, Bill Greene, John Tlumacki, Bill Polo, George Riley, John Blanding, Joanne Rathe, Suzanne Kreiter, John Ioven, Jim Davis, Wendy Maeda, Pat Greenhouse, Tom Landers, Frank O'Brien, Jonathan Wiggs, George Rizer, Barry Chin, Essdras Suarez, Evan Richman, Maureen O'Brien, and Ellen Clegg.

And many thanks to those talented imaging technicians: Susan Chalifoux, Janine Rodenhiser and Cindy Meloski.

I want to acknowledge and thank: Brian McDonough, Janice and John Schneiderman, Bob Collins, Bob Madden, Mark Shanahan, Meredith Goldstein, Bob Devine, Joe Davey, Tom Lacey, Corrine and Ricky Ball, David Ting, Jack Doherty, Joe Foley, Jodi Bulman, Kathleen Hickey, Steve Owens, Jan Goldstein, Ed Hayward, Don Perrin, Ed Smith, John McDermott, Bill and Ed Forry, Peter Brown, Bill and Ed Balas, Marshall, Barry and Linda Sloan, Pat Beggy, Jan Saragoni, Ellie Hart, Jim Flynn, Joe Finn, Doreen Vigue, Jean Carter, Scott Lundgren, Mary Mulvey, Doc Walsh, Bob Taveres, Barbara Huebner, Kirsten Ripple, Genevieve Hemenway, Chris Chilopi, Steve Charbonnier, Skip Toomey, Dan McDonald, Steve MacDonald, Brian Doherty, Bridie Doherty, Kathy Keefe, Marge Dooley, Bob Bingham, Catherine Nelson, Richie Parrish, Mike, Neal and Bo Mullane, Bob Long, Kevin Honan, Pat Kelly, Rosalie Ware, Paul LeBlanc, John Naughton, Jim Wyse, Elaine Driscoll, and Dan Keeler for their support.

Also: Colm Lydon, Tim Horan, Boston Police Superintendent in Chief Willie Gross, Ben Bradlee, Jr., Ed Buckley, Ed Bulger, Peter Casey, Jack Cullen, Jack Danilecki, Bob Dougherty, Chris Burke, Michele McPhee, Bill McQuillan, Christine McSherry, Jim and Michael Morris, Paul O'Connor, Gregg Nolan, Megan O'Toole, Jim Quirk, Devon Miller, Stacey Geezil, Emily McDonough, Kristen Manning, Jen Shea, Bob Manning, Leona Dunphy and her mother Linda, Barbara Courtney, Carole Brennan, Marjorie O'Donnell, Marjorie Clapprood, Andy McCarthy, Bonnie Edes, Bruce Wheltle, Jim Concannon, Jayne Larson, Tom McIntyre, Sr., Erin Lambe, Katie Edwards, Katherine Contos, Karen and Jimmy Klidaras, Elaine Delaney, Maxine and Anthony Klidaras, Chris Roche and his daughter Shannon, and Winnie Cotter. Your support and contributions have been instrumental to the publication of this book.

Special thanks are due to Jennifer Hill and Mark Duffield, who introduced me to the founders and inspiring women at Three Bean Press—our publishers, whose guidance, creativity, and professionalism once again made for a terrific publishing experience.

—Bill Brett

INDEX